Mineral Resources, Grade 11

T0383801

What if you could challenge your eleventh graders to come up with a design solution for developing, managing, and utilizing mineral resources? With this volume in the *STEM Road Map Curriculum Series*, you can!

Mineral Resources outlines a journey that will steer your students toward authentic problem solving while grounding them in integrated STEM disciplines. Like the other volumes in the series, this book is designed to meet the growing need to infuse real-world learning into K–12 classrooms.

This interdisciplinary, three-lesson module uses project- and problem-based learning to help students develop an in-depth understanding of mineral resources by researching the utility and impact of particular mineral resources on society. Working in teams, students will locate quantitative and qualitative data on mineral resources and discern the reliability of the information, then use their data to write an opinion article and develop a website to convince readers of the effectiveness of a particular design solution for developing, managing, and utilizing mineral resources. To support this goal, students will do the following:

- Explain how mineral resources are located and used in various ways in society.

- Explain why mineral resources are important to society.

- Critically evaluate quantitative and qualitative data about mineral resources.

- Write an opinion article demonstrating their knowledge about competing design solutions for extracting mineral resources.

The *STEM Road Map Curriculum Series* is anchored in the Next Generation Science Standards, the Common Core State Standards, and the Framework for 21st Century Learning. In-depth and flexible, *Mineral Resources* can be used as a whole unit or in part to meet the needs of districts, schools, and teachers who are charting a course toward an integrated STEM approach.

Carla C. Johnson is Professor of Science Education in the College of Education and Office of Research and Innovation, and a Faculty Research Fellow at North Carolina State University in North Carolina, USA

Janet B. Walton is Senior Research Scholar at North Carolina State University in North Carolina, USA

Erin E. Peters-Burton is the Donna R. and David E. Sterling Endowed Professor in Science Education at George Mason University in Virginia, USA

STEM ROAD MAP CURRICULUM SERIES

Series editors: Carla C. Johnson, Janet B. Walton, and Erin E. Peters-Burton

Map out a journey that will steer your students toward authentic problem solving as you ground them in integrated STEM disciplines.

Co-published by Routledge and NSTA Press, in partnership with the National Science Teaching Association, this K–12 curriculum series is anchored in the Next Generation Science Standards, the Common Core State Standards, and the Framework for 21st Century Learning. It was developed to meet the growing need to infuse real-world STEM learning into classrooms.

Each book is an in-depth module that uses project- and problem-based learning. First, your students are presented with a challenge. Then, they apply what they learn using science, social studies, English language arts, and mathematics. Engaging and flexible, each volume can be used as a whole unit or in part to meet the needs of districts, schools, and teachers who are charting a course toward an integrated STEM approach.

Modules are available from NSTA Press and Routledge, and organized under the following themes. For an update listing of the volumes in the series, please visit https://www.routledge.com/STEM-Road-Map-Curriculum-Series/book-series/SRM (for titles co-published by Routledge and NSTA Press), or www.nsta.org/book-series/stem-road-map-curriculum (for titles published by NSTA Press).

Co-published by Routledge and NSTA Press:

Optimizing the Human Experience:

- *Our Changing Environment, Grade K: STEM Road Map for Elementary School*
- *Genetically Modified Organisms, Grade 7: STEM Road Map for Middle School*
- *Rebuilding the Natural Environment, Grade 10: STEM Road Map for High School*
- *Mineral Resources, Grade 11: STEM Road Map for High School*

Cause and Effect:

- *Formation of the Earth, Grade 9: STEM Road Map for High School*

Published by NSTA Press:

Innovation and Progress:

- *Amusement Park of the Future, Grade 6: STEM Road Map for Elementary School*
- *Transportation in the Future, Grade 3: STEM Road Map for Elementary School*
- *Harnessing Solar Energy, Grade 4: STEM Road Map for Elementary School*
- *Wind Energy, Grade 5: STEM Road Map for Elementary School*
- *Construction Materials, Grade 11: STEM Road Map for High School*

The Represented World:

- *Patterns and the Plant World, Grade 1: STEM Road Map for Elementary School*
- *Investigating Environmental Changes, Grade 2: STEM Road Map for Elementary School*

- *Swing Set Makeover, Grade 3: STEM Road Map for Elementary School*
- *Rainwater Analysis, Grade 5: STEM Road Map for Elementary School*
- *Packaging Design, Grade 6: STEM Road Map for Middle School*
- *Improving Bridge Design, Grade 8: STEM Road Map for Middle School*
- *Radioactivity, Grade 11: STEM Road Map for High School*
- *Car Crashes, Grade 12: STEM Road Map for High School*

Cause and Effect:

- *Physics in Motion, Grade K: STEM Road Map for Elementary School*
- *Influence of Waves, Grade 1: STEM Road Map for Elementary School*
- *Natural Hazards, Grade 2: STEM Road Map for Elementary School*
- *Human Impacts on Our Climate, Grade 6: STEM Road Map for Middle School*
- *The Changing Earth, Grade 8: STEM Road Map for Middle School*
- *Healthy Living, Grade 10: STEM Road Map for High School*

Mineral Resources

Grade 11

STEM Road Map for High School

Edited by Carla C. Johnson, Janet B. Walton, and
Erin E. Peters-Burton

Routledge
Taylor & Francis Group

NEW YORK AND LONDON

nsta Press
National Science Teaching Association

Cover images: icon © Shutterstock, map © Getty Images
Art and design for cover and interior adapted from NSTA Press.

First published 2022
by Routledge
605 Third Avenue, New York, NY 10158

and by Routledge
4 Park Square, Milton Park, Abingdon, Oxon, OX14 4RN

Routledge is an imprint of the Taylor & Francis Group, an informa business

A co-publication with NSTA Press.

Library of Congress Cataloging-in-Publication Data
Names: Johnson, Carla C., 1969– editor. | Walton, Janet B., 1968– editor. | Peters-Burton, Erin E., editor.
Title: Mineral resources grade 11 : STEM road map for high school / edited by Carla C. Johnson, Janet B. Walton, and Erin E. Peters Burton.
Description: New York, NY : Routledge, 2022. | Series: Stem road map curriculum series | Includes bibliographical references and index.
Identifiers: LCCN 2021053245 | ISBN 9781032199887 (hardback) | ISBN 9781032199870 (paperback) | ISBN 9781003261742 (ebook)
Subjects: LCSH: Mines and mineral resources. | Eleventh grade (Education)
Classification: LCC TN148 .M56 2022 | DDC 333.8/5—dc23/eng/20220103
LC record available at https://lccn.loc.gov/2021053245

ISBN: 978-1-032-19988-7 (hbk)
ISBN: 978-1-032-19987-0 (pbk)
ISBN: 978-1-003-26174-2 (ebk)

DOI: 10.4324/9781003261742

Typeset in Palatino LT Std
by Apex CoVantage, LLC

CONTENTS

Part 1: The STEM Road Map: Background, Theory, and Practice

① Overview of the *STEM Road Map Curriculum Series* 1

Carla C. Johnson, Erin E. Peters-Burton, and Tamara J. Moore

② Strategies Used in the *STEM Road Map Curriculum Series* 9

*Erin E. Peters-Burton, Carla C. Johnson, Toni A. May, and
Tamara J. Moore*

Part 2: Mineral Resources: STEM Road Map Module

③ Mineral Resources Module Overview 25

*Erin E. Peters-Burton, Giuseppina Mattietti, Jennifer Drake
Patrick, Brad Rankin, Anthony Pellegrino, Susan Poland,
Janet B. Walton, and Carla C. Johnson*

CONTENTS

*Erin E. Peters-Burton, Giuseppina Mattietti, Jennifer Drake-Patrick,
Brad Rankin, Anthony Pellegrino, Susan Poland, Janet B. Walton,
and Carla C. Johnson*

Carla C. Johnson

ABOUT THE EDITORS AND AUTHORS

Dr. Carla C. Johnson is a Professor of Science Education and Office of Research and Innovation Faculty Research Fellow at NC State University. Dr. Johnson has served (2015–2021) as the director of research and evaluation for the Department of Defense–funded Army Educational Outreach Program (AEOP), a global portfolio of STEM education programs, competitions, and apprenticeships. She has been a leader in STEM education for the past decade, serving as the director of STEM Centers, editor of the *School Science and Mathematics* journal, and lead researcher for the evaluation of Tennessee's Race to the Top–funded STEM portfolio. Dr. Johnson has published over 200 articles, books, book chapters, and curriculum books focused on STEM education. She is a former science and social studies teacher and was the recipient of the 2013 Outstanding Science Teacher Educator of the Year award from the Association for Science Teacher Education (ASTE), the 2012 Award for Excellence in Integrating Science and Mathematics from the School Science and Mathematics Association (SSMA), the 2014 award for best paper on Implications of Research for Educational Practice from ASTE, and the 2006 Outstanding Early Career Scholar Award from SSMA. Her research focuses on STEM education policy implementation, effective science teaching, and integrated STEM approaches.

Dr. Janet B. Walton is a Senior Research Scholar at NC State's College of Education in Raleigh, North Carolina. Formerly the STEM workforce program manager for Virginia's Region 2000 and founding director of the Future Focus Foundation, a nonprofit organization dedicated to enhancing the quality of STEM education in the region, she merges her economic development and education backgrounds to develop K–12 curricular materials that integrate real-life issues with sound cross-curricular content. Her research focus includes collaboration between schools and community stakeholders for STEM education, problem- and project-based learning pedagogies, online learning, and mixed methods research methodologies. She leverages this background to bring contextual STEM experiences into the classroom and provide students and educators with innovative resources and curricular materials. She is the former assistant director of evaluation of research and evaluation for the Department of Defense-funded Army Educational Outreach Program (AEOP), a global portfolio of STEM education programs, competitions, and apprenticeships and specializes in evaluation of STEM programs.

Dr. Erin E. Peters-Burton is the Donna R. and David E. Sterling Endowed Professor in Science Education at George Mason University in Fairfax, Virginia. She uses her experiences from 15 years as an engineer and secondary science, engineering, and mathematics teacher to develop research projects that directly inform classroom practice in science and engineering. Her research agenda is based on the idea that all students should build self-awareness of how they learn science and engineering. She works to help students see themselves as "science-minded" and help teachers create classrooms that support student skills to develop scientific knowledge. To accomplish this, she pursues research projects that investigate ways that students and teachers can use self-regulated learning theory in science and engineering, as well as how inclusive STEM schools can help students succeed. During her tenure as a secondary teacher, she had a National Board Certification in Early Adolescent Science and was an Albert Einstein Distinguished Educator Fellow for NASA. As a researcher, Dr. Peters-Burton has published over 100 articles, books, book chapters, and curriculum books focused on STEM education and educational psychology. She received the Outstanding Science Teacher Educator of the Year award from ASTE in 2016 and a Teacher of Distinction Award and a Scholarly Achievement Award from George Mason University in 2012, and in 2010 she was named University Science Educator of the Year by the Virginia Association of Science Teachers.

Dr. Guiseppina Mattietti is an Assistant Professor of Earth Science in the Department of Atmospheric, Oceanic and Earth George Mason University. Kysar Mattietti, received a BS in Earth Science and worked as a teacher of mathematics and science in high school and then as junior researcher at the National Institute of Geophysics in her native city of Rome, Italy, before going to graduate school in the US. She obtained a PhD in Earth Science with a focus on Caribbean Geology at George Washington University. She worked for eight years in the Department of Mineral Sciences at the Smithsonian Institution where she became interested in teaching for everybody in informal settings.

Dr. Andrea R. Milner is the vice president and dean of academic affairs and an associate professor in the Teacher Education Department at Adrian College in Adrian, Michigan. A former early childhood and elementary teacher, Dr. Milner researches the effects constructivist classroom contextual factors have on student motivation and learning strategy use.

Dr. Tamara J. Moore is an associate professor of engineering education in the College of Engineering at Purdue University. Dr. Moore's research focuses on defining STEM integration through the use of engineering as the connection and investigating its power for student learning.

Dr. Vanessa B. Morrison is an associate professor in the Teacher Education Department at Adrian College. She is a former early childhood teacher and reading and language arts specialist whose research is focused on learning and teaching within a transdisciplinary framework.

Dr. Toni A. May is an associate professor of assessment, research, and statistics in the School of Education at Drexel University in Philadelphia. Dr. May's research concentrates on assessment and evaluation in education, with a focus on K–12 STEM.

Dr. Jennifer Drake Patrick is an assistant professor of literacy education in the College of Education and Human Development at George Mason University. A former English language arts teacher, she focuses her research on disciplinary literacy.

Dr. Anthony Pellegrino is an assistant professor of social science in the College of Education at The University of Tennessee, Knoxville. He is a former social studies and history teacher whose research interests include youth-centered pedagogies and social science teacher preparation.

Dr. Bradley D. Rankin is a high school mathematics teacher at Wakefield High School in Arlington, Virginia. He has been teaching mathematics for 20 years, is board certified, and has a PhD in mathematics education leadership from George Mason University.

Dr. Susan Poland is a PhD student and Presidential Scholar at George Mason University focusing in science education research. With an undergraduate degree in integrated science education and a master's degree in curriculum and instruction focusing on STEM education, Susan has taught elementary, middle, and high school courses in engineering and all domains of science. Her research in the PhD program focuses on the enactment of scientific research in the classroom.

ACKNOWLEDGMENTS

This module was developed as a part of the STEM Road Map project (Carla C. Johnson, principal investigator). The Purdue University College of Education, General Motors, and other sources provided funding for this project.

See *www.routledge.com/9781138804234* for more information about *STEM Road Map: A Framework for Integrated STEM Education*.

PART 1

THE STEM ROAD MAP

BACKGROUND, THEORY, AND PRACTICE

OVERVIEW OF THE *STEM ROAD MAP CURRICULUM SERIES*

Carla C. Johnson, Erin E. Peters-Burton, and Tamara J. Moore

The *STEM Road Map Curriculum Series* was conceptualized and developed by a team of STEM educators from across the United States in response to a growing need to infuse real-world learning contexts, delivered through authentic problem-solving pedagogy, into K–12 classrooms. The curriculum series is grounded in integrated STEM, which focuses on the integration of the STEM disciplines – science, technology, engineering, and mathematics – delivered across content areas, incorporating the Framework for 21st Century Learning along with grade-level-appropriate academic standards. The curriculum series begins in kindergarten, with a five-week instructional sequence that introduces students to the STEM themes and gives them grade-level-appropriate topics and real-world challenges or problems to solve. The series uses project-based and problem-based learning, presenting students with the problem or challenge during the first lesson, and then teaching them science, social studies, English language arts, mathematics, and other content, as they apply what they learn to the challenge or problem at hand.

Authentic assessment and differentiation are embedded throughout the modules. Each *STEM Road Map Curriculum Series* module has a lead discipline, which may be science, social studies, English language arts, or mathematics. All disciplines are integrated into each module, along with ties to engineering. Another key component is the use of STEM Research Notebooks to allow students to track their own learning progress. The modules are designed with a scaffolded approach, with increasingly complex concepts and skills introduced as students' progress through grade levels.

The developers of this work view the curriculum as a resource that is intended to be used either as a whole or in part to meet the needs of districts, schools, and teachers who are implementing an integrated STEM approach. A variety of implementation formats are possible, from using one stand- alone module at a given grade level to using all five modules to provide 25 weeks of instruction. Also, within each grade

DOI: 10.4324/9781003261742-2

band (K–2, 3–5, 6–8, 9–12), the modules can be sequenced in various ways to suit specific needs.

STANDARDS-BASED APPROACH

The *STEM Road Map Curriculum Series* is anchored in the *Next Generation Science Standards* (*NGSS*), the *Common Core State Standards for Mathematics* (*CCSS Mathematics*), the *Common Core State Standards for English Language Arts* (*CCSS ELA*), and the Framework for 21st Century Learning. Each module includes a detailed curriculum map that incorporates the associated standards from the particular area correlated to lesson plans. The STEM Road Map has very clear and strong connections to these academic standards, and each of the grade-level topics was derived from the mapping of the standards to ensure alignment among topics, challenges or problems, and the required academic standards for students. Therefore, the curriculum series takes a standards-based approach and is designed to provide authentic contexts for application of required knowledge and skills.

THEMES IN THE *STEM ROAD MAP CURRICULUM SERIES*

The K–12 STEM Road Map is organized around five real-world STEM themes that were generated through an examination of the big ideas and challenges for society included in STEM standards and those that are persistent dilemmas for current and future generations:

- Cause and Effect
- Innovation and Progress
- The Represented World
- Sustainable Systems
- Optimizing the Human Experience

These themes are designed as springboards for launching students into an exploration of real-world learning situated within big ideas. Most important, the five STEM Road Map themes serve as a framework for scaffolding STEM learning across the K–12 continuum.

The themes are distributed across the STEM disciplines so that they represent the big ideas in science (Cause and Effect; Sustainable Systems), technology (Innovation and Progress; Optimizing the Human Experience), engineering (Innovation and Progress; Sustainable Systems; Optimizing the Human Experience), and mathematics (The Rep- resented World), as well as concepts and challenges in social studies and 21st century skills that are also excellent contexts for learning in English language arts. The process of developing themes began with the clustering of the *NGSS* performance expectations and the National Academy of Engineering's grand challenges for engineering, which led to the development of the challenge in each module and connections of the module activities to the *CCSS Mathematics* and *CCSS ELA* standards. We performed these mapping processes with large teams of experts and found that these five themes pro- vided breadth, depth, and coherence to frame a high-quality STEM learning experience from kindergarten through 12th grade.

Cause and Effect

The concept of cause and effect is a powerful and pervasive notion in the STEM fields. It is the foundation of understanding how and why things happen as they do. Humans spend considerable effort and resources trying to understand the causes and effects of natural and designed phenomena to gain better control over events and the environment and to be prepared to react appropriately. Equipped with the knowledge of a specific cause-and-effect relationship, we can lead better lives or contribute to the community by altering the cause, leading to a different effect. For example, if a person recognizes that irresponsible energy consumption leads to global climate change, that person can act to remedy his or her contribution to the situation. Although cause and effect is a core idea in the STEM fields, it can actually be difficult to determine. Students should be capable of understanding not only when evidence points to cause and effect but also when evidence points to relationships but not direct causality. The major goal of education is to foster students to be empowered, analytic thinkers, capable of thinking through complex processes to make important decisions. Understanding causality, as well as when it cannot be determined, will help students become better consumers, global citizens, and community members.

Innovation and Progress

One of the most important factors in determining whether humans will have a positive future is innovation. Innovation is the driving force behind progress, which helps create possibilities that did not exist before. Innovation and progress are creative entities, but in the STEM fields, they are anchored by evidence and logic, and they use established concepts to move the STEM fields forward. In creating something new, students must consider what is already known in the STEM fields and apply this knowledge appropriately. When we innovate, we create value that was not there previously and create new conditions and possibilities for even more innovations. Students should consider how their innovations might affect progress and use their STEM thinking to change current human burdens to benefits. For example, if we develop more efficient cars that use by-products from another manufacturing industry, such as food processing, then we have used waste productively and reduced the need for the waste to be hauled away, an indirect benefit of the innovation.

The Represented World

When we communicate about the world we live in, how the world works, and how we can meet the needs of humans, sometimes we can use the actual phenomena to explain a concept. Sometimes, however, the concept is too big, too slow, too small, too fast, or too complex for us to explain using the actual phenomena, and we must use a representation or a model to help communicate the important features. We need representations and models such as graphs, tables, mathematical expressions, and diagrams because it makes our thinking visible. For example, when examining geologic time, we cannot actually observe the passage of such large chunks of time, so we create a timeline or a model that uses a proportional scale to visually illustrate how much time has passed for different eras. Another example may be something too complex for students at a particular grade level, such as explaining the p subshell orbitals of electrons to fifth graders. Instead, we use the Bohr model, which more closely represents the orbiting of planets and is accessible to fifth graders.

When we create models, they are helpful because they point out the most important features of a phenomenon. We also create representations of the world with mathematical functions, which help us change parameters to suit the situation. Creating representations of a phenomenon engages students because they are able to identify the important features of that phenomenon and communicate them directly. But because models are estimates of a phenomenon, they leave out some of the details, so it is important for students to evaluate their usefulness as well as their shortcomings.

Sustainable Systems

From an engineering perspective, the term *system* refers to the use of "concepts of component need, component interaction, systems interaction, and feedback. The interaction of subcomponents to produce a functional system is a common lens used by all engineering disciplines for understanding, analysis, and design." (Koehler, Bloom, and Binns 2013, p. 8). Systems can be either open (e.g., an ecosystem) or closed (e.g., a car battery). Ideally, a system should be sustainable, able to maintain equilibrium without much energy from outside the structure. Looking at a garden, we see flowers blooming, weeds sprouting, insects buzzing, and various forms of life living within its boundaries. This is an example of an ecosystem, a collection of living organisms that survive together, functioning as a system. The interaction of the organisms within the system and the influences of the environment (e.g., water, sunlight) can maintain the system for a period of time, thus demonstrating its ability to endure. Sustainability is a desirable feature of a system because it allows for existence of the entity in the long term.

In the STEM Road Map project, we identified different standards that we consider to be oriented toward systems that students should know and understand in the K–12 setting. These include ecosystems, the rock cycle, Earth processes (such as erosion, tectonics, ocean currents, weather phenomena), Earth-Sun-Moon cycles, heat transfer, and the interaction among the geosphere, biosphere, hydrosphere, and atmosphere. Students and teachers should understand that we live in a world of systems that are not independent of each other, but rather are intrinsically linked such that a disruption in one part of a system will have reverberating effects on other parts of the system.

Optimizing the Human Experience

Science, technology, engineering, and mathematics as disciplines have the capacity to continuously improve the ways humans live, interact, and find meaning in the world, thus working to optimize the human experience. This idea has two components: being more suited to our environment and being more fully human. For example, the progression of STEM ideas can help humans create solutions to complex problems, such as improving ways to access water sources, designing energy sources with minimal impact on our environment, developing new ways of communication and expression, and building efficient shelters. STEM ideas can also provide access to the secrets and wonders of nature. Learning in STEM requires students to think logically and systematically, which is a way of knowing the world that is markedly different from knowing the world as an artist. When students can employ various ways of knowing and understand when it is appropriate to use a different way of knowing or integrate ways of knowing, they are fully experiencing the best of what it is to be human. The problem-based learning scenarios provided in the STEM Road Map help students develop ways of thinking like STEM professionals as they ask questions and design solutions. They learn to optimize the human experience by innovating improvements in the designed world in which they live.

THE NEED FOR AN INTEGRATED STEM APPROACH

At a basic level, STEM stands for science, technology, engineering, and mathematics. Over the past decade, however, STEM has evolved to have a much broader scope and implications. Now, educators and policy makers refer to STEM as not only a concentrated area for investing in the future of the United States and other nations but also as a domain and mechanism for educational reform. The good intentions of the recent decade-plus of focus on accountability and increased testing has resulted in significant decreases not only in instructional time for teaching science and social studies but also in the flexibility of teachers to promote authentic, problem solving–focused classroom environments. The shift has had a detrimental impact on student acquisition of vitally important skills, which many refer to as 21st century skills, and often the ability of students to "think." Further, schooling has become increasingly siloed into compartments of mathematics, science, English language, arts and social studies, lacking any of the

connections that are overwhelmingly present in the real world around children. Students have experienced school as content provided in boxes that must be memorized, devoid of any real-world context, and often have little understanding of why they are learning these things.

STEM-focused projects, curriculum, activities, and schools have emerged as a means to address these challenges. However, most of these efforts have continued to focus on the individual STEM disciplines (predominantly science and engineering) through more STEM classes and after-school programs in a "STEM enhanced" approach (Breiner et al. 2012). But in traditional and STEM enhanced approaches, there is little to no focus on other disciplines that are integral to the context of STEM in the real world. Integrated STEM education, on the other hand, infuses the learning of important STEM content and concepts with a much-needed emphasis on 21st century skills and a problem- and project-based pedagogy that more closely mirrors the real-world setting for society's challenges. It incorporates social studies, English language arts, and the arts as pivotal and necessary (Johnson 2013; Rennie, Venville, and Wallace 2012; Roehrig et al. 2012).

Framework for Stem Integration in The Classroom

The *STEM Road Map Curriculum Series* is grounded in the Framework for STEM Integration in the Classroom as conceptualized by Moore, Guzey, and Brown (2014) and Moore et al. (2014). The framework has six elements, described in the context of how they are used in the *STEM Road Map Curriculum Series* as follows:

1. The STEM Road Map contexts are meaningful to students and provide motivation to engage with the content. Together, these allow students to have different ways to enter into the challenge.

2. The STEM Road Map modules include engineering design that allows students to design technologies (i.e., products that are part of the designed world) for a compelling purpose.

3. The STEM Road Map modules provide students with the opportunities to learn from failure and redesign based on the lessons learned.

4. The STEM Road Map modules include standards-based disciplinary content as the learning objectives.

5. The STEM Road Map modules include student-centered pedagogies that allow students to grapple with the content, tie their ideas to the context, and learn to think for themselves as they deepen their conceptual knowledge.

6. The STEM Road Map modules emphasize 21st century skills and, in particular, highlight communication and teamwork.

All of the STEM Road Map modules incorporate these six elements; however, the level of emphasis on each of these elements varies based on the challenge or problem in each module.

THE NEED FOR THE *STEM ROAD MAP CURRICULUM SERIES*

As focus is increasing on integrated STEM, and additional schools and programs decide to move their curriculum and instruction in this direction, there is a need for high- quality, research-based curriculum designed with integrated STEM at the core. Several good resources are available to help teachers infuse engineering or more STEM enhanced approaches, but no curriculum exists that spans K–12 with an integrated STEM focus. The next chapter provides detailed information about the specific pedagogy, instructional strategies, and learning theory on which the *STEM Road Map Curriculum Series* is grounded.

REFERENCES

Breiner, J., M. Harkness, C. C. Johnson, and C. Koehler. 2012. What is STEM? A discussion about conceptions of STEM in education and partnerships. *School Science and Mathematics* 112 (1): 3–11.

Johnson, C. C. 2013. Conceptualizing integrated STEM education: Editorial. *School Science and Mathematics* 113 (8): 367–368.

Koehler, C. M., M. A. Bloom, and I. C. Binns. 2013. Lights, camera, action: Developing a methodology to document mainstream films' portrayal of nature of science and scientific inquiry. *Electronic Journal of Science Education* 17 (2).

Moore, T. J., S. S. Guzey, and A. Brown. 2014. Greenhouse design to increase habitable land: An engineering unit. *Science Scope* 51–57.

Moore, T. J., M. S. Stohlmann, H.-H. Wang, K. M. Tank, A. W. Glancy, and G. H. Roehrig. 2014. Implementation and integration of engineering in K–12 STEM education. In *Engineering in pre- college settings: Synthesizing research, policy, and practices,* ed. S. Purzer, J. Strobel, and M. Cardella, 35–60. West Lafayette, IN: Purdue Press.

Rennie, L., G. Venville, and J. Wallace. 2012. *Integrating science, technology, engineering, and mathematics: Issues, reflections, and ways forward.* New York: Routledge.

Roehrig, G. H., T. J. Moore, H. H. Wang, and M. S. Park. 2012. Is adding the *E* enough? Investigating the impact of K–12 engineering standards on the implementation of STEM integration. *School Science and Mathematics* 112 (1): 31–44.

STRATEGIES USED IN THE *STEM ROAD MAP CURRICULUM SERIES*

Erin E. Peters-Burton, Carla C. Johnson, Toni A. May, and Tamara J. Moore

The *STEM Road Map Curriculum Series* uses what has been identified through research as best-practice pedagogy, including embedded formative assessment strategies throughout each module. This chapter briefly describes the key strategies that are employed in the series.

PROJECT- AND PROBLEM-BASED LEARNING

Each module in the *STEM Road Map Curriculum Series* uses either project-based learning or problem-based learning to drive the instruction. Project-based learning begins with a driving question to guide student teams in addressing a contextualized local or com- munity problem or issue. The outcome of project-based instruction is a product that is conceptualized, designed, and tested through a series of scaffolded learning experiences (Blumenfeld et al. 1991; Krajcik and Blumenfeld 2006). Problem-based learning is often grounded in a fictitious scenario, challenge, or problem (Barell 2006; Lambros 2004). On the first day of instruction within the unit, student teams are provided with the context of the problem. Teams work through a series of activities and use open-ended research to develop their potential solution to the problem or challenge, which need not be a tangible product (Johnson 2003).

ENGINEERING DESIGN PROCESS

The *STEM Road Map Curriculum Series* uses engineering design as a way to facilitate integrated STEM within the modules. The engineering design process (EDP) is depicted in Figure 2.1 (p. 10). It highlights two major aspects of engineering design – problem scoping and solution generation – and six specific components of

DOI: 10.4324/9781003261742-3

Figure 2.1. Engineering Design Process

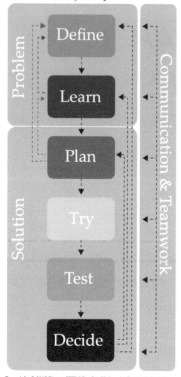

Engineering Design Process
A way to improve

Copyright © 2015 PictureSTEM-Purdue University Research Foundation

working toward a design: define the problem, learn about the problem, plan a solution, try the solution, test the solution, decide whether the solution is good enough. It also shows that communication and teamwork are involved throughout the entire process. As the arrows in the figure indicate, the order in which the components of engineering design are addressed depends on what becomes needed as designers progress through the EDP. Designers must communicate and work in teams throughout the process. The EDP is iterative, meaning that components of the process can be repeated as needed until the design is good enough to present to the client as a potential solution to the problem.

Problem scoping is the process of gathering and analyzing information to deeply understand the engineering design problem. It includes defining the problem and learning about the problem. Defining the problem includes identifying the problem, the client, and the end user of the design. The client is the person (or people) who hired the designers to do the work, and the end user is the person (or people) who will use the final design. The designers must also identify the criteria and the constraints of the problem. The criteria are the things the client wants from the solution, and the constraints are the things that limit the possible solutions. The designers must spend significant time learning about the problem, which can include activities such as the following:

- Reading informational texts and researching about relevant concepts or contexts

- Identifying and learning about needed mathematical and scientific skills, knowledge, and tools

- Learning about things done previously to solve similar problems

- Experimenting with possible materials that could be used in the design

Problem scoping also allows designers to consider how to measure the success of the design in addressing specific criteria and staying within the constraints over multiple iterations of solution generation.

Solution generation includes planning a solution, trying the solution, testing the solution, and deciding whether the solution is good enough. Planning the solution includes generating many design ideas that both address the criteria and meet the constraints. Here the designers must consider what was learned about the problem during problem scoping. Design plans include clear communication of design ideas through media such as notebooks, blueprints, schematics, or storyboards. They also include details about the design, such as measurements, materials, colors, costs of materials, instructions for how things fit together, and sets of directions. Making the decision about which design idea to move forward involves considering the trade-offs of each design idea.

Once a clear design plan is in place, the designers must try the solution. Trying the solution includes developing a prototype (a testable model) based on the plan generated. The prototype might be something physical or a process to accomplish a goal. This com- ponent of design requires that the designers consider the risk involved in implementing the design. The prototype developed must be tested. Testing the solution includes con- ducting fair tests that verify whether the plan is a solution that is good enough to meet the client and end user needs and wants. Data need to be collected about the results of the tests of the prototype, and these data should be used to make evidence-based decisions regarding the design choices made in the plan. Here, the designers must again consider the criteria and constraints for the problem.

Using the data gathered from the testing, the designers must decide whether the solution is good enough to meet the client and end user needs and wants by assessment based on the criteria and constraints. Here, the designers must justify or reject design decisions based on the background research gathered while learning about the problem and on the evidence gathered during the testing of the solution. The designers must now decide whether to present the current solution to the client as a possibility or to do more iterations of design on the solution. If they decide that improvements need to be made to the solution, the designers must decide if there is more that needs to be understood about the problem, client, or end user; if another design idea should be tried; or if more planning needs to be conducted on the same design. One way or another, more work needs to be done.

Throughout the process of designing a solution to meet a client's needs and wants, designers work in teams and must communicate to each other, the client, and likely the end user. Teamwork is important in engineering design because multiple perspectives and differing skills and knowledge are valuable when working to solve problems. Communication is key to the success of the designed solution. Designers must communicate their ideas clearly using many different representations, such as text in an engineering notebook, diagrams, flowcharts, technical briefs, or memos to the client.

LEARNING CYCLE

The same format for the learning cycle is used in all grade levels throughout the STEM Road Map, so that students engage in a variety of activities to learn about phenomena in the modules thoroughly and have consistent experiences in the problem- and

project- based learning modules. Expectations for learning by younger students are not as high as for older students, but the format of the progression of learning is the same. Students who have learned with curriculum from the STEM Road Map in early grades know what to expect in later grades. The learning cycle consists of five parts – Introductory Activity/Engagement, Activity/Exploration, Explanation, Elaboration/ Application of Knowledge, and Evaluation/Assessment – and is based on the empirically tested 5E model from BSCS (Bybee et al. 2006).

In the Introductory Activity/Engagement phase, teachers introduce the module challenge and use a unique approach designed to pique students' curiosity. This phase gets students to start thinking about what they already know about the topic and begin wondering about key ideas. The Introductory Activity/Engagement phase positions students to be confident about what they are about to learn, because they have prior knowledge, and clues them into what they don't yet know.

In the Activity/Exploration phase, the teacher sets up activities in which students experience a deeper look at the topics that were introduced earlier. Students engage in the activities and generate new questions or consider possibilities using preliminary investigations. Students work independently, in small groups, and in whole-group settings to conduct investigations, resulting in common experiences about the topic and skills involved in the real-world activities. Teachers can assess students' development of concepts and skills based on the common experiences during this phase.

During the Explanation phase, teachers direct students' attention to concepts they need to understand and skills they need to possess to accomplish the challenge. Students participate in activities to demonstrate their knowledge and skills to this point, and teachers can pinpoint gaps in student knowledge during this phase.

In the Elaboration/Application of Knowledge phase, teachers present students with activities that engage in higher-order thinking to create depth and breadth of student knowledge, while connecting ideas across topics within and across STEM. Students apply what they have learned thus far in the module to a new context or elaborate on what they have learned about the topic to a deeper level of detail.

In the last phase, Evaluation/Assessment, teachers give students summative feedback on their knowledge and skills as demonstrated through the challenge. This is not the only point of assessment (as discussed in the section on Embedded Formative Assessments), but it is an assessment of the culmination of the knowledge and skills for the module. Students demonstrate their cognitive growth at this point and reflect on how far they have come since the beginning of the module. The challenges are designed to be multidimensional in the ways students must collaborate and communicate their new knowledge.

STEM RESEARCH NOTEBOOK

One of the main components of the *STEM Road Map Curriculum Series* is the STEM Research Notebook, a place for students to capture their ideas, questions, observations, reflections, evidence of progress, and other items associated with their daily work. At the beginning of each module, the teacher walks students through the setup of the STEM Research Notebook, which could be a three-ring binder, composition book, or spiral notebook. You may wish to have students create divided sections so that they can easily access work from various disciplines during the module. Electronic notebooks kept on student devices are also acceptable and encouraged. Students will develop their own table of contents and create chapters in the notebook for each module.

Each lesson in the *STEM Road Map Curriculum Series* includes one or more prompts that are designed for inclusion in the STEM Research Notebook and appear as questions or statements that the teacher assigns to students. These prompts require students to apply what they have learned across the lesson to solve the big problem or challenge for that module. Each lesson is designed to meaningfully refer students to the larger problem or challenge they have been assigned to solve with their teams. The STEM Research Notebook is designed to be a key formative assessment tool, as students' daily entries provide evidence of what they are learning. The notebook can be used as a mechanism for dialogue between the teacher and students, as well as for peer and self-evaluation.

The use of the STEM Research Notebook is designed to scaffold student notebooking skills across the grade bands in the *STEM Road Map Curriculum Series*. In the early grades, children learn how to organize their daily work in the notebook as a way to collect their products for future reference. In elementary school, students structure their notebooks to integrate background research along with their daily work and lesson prompts. In the upper grades (middle and high school), students expand their use of research and data gathering through team discussions to more closely mirror the work of STEM experts in the real world.

THE ROLE OF ASSESSMENT IN THE *STEM ROAD MAP CURRICULUM SERIES*

Starting in the middle years and continuing into secondary education, the word *assessment* typically brings grades to mind. These grades may take the form of a letter or a percentage, but they typically are used as a representation of a student's content mastery. If well thought out and implemented, however, classroom assessment can offer teachers, parents, and students valuable information about student learning and misconceptions that does not necessarily come in the form of a grade (Popham 2013).

The *STEM Road Map Curriculum Series* provides a set of assessments for each module. Teachers are encouraged to use assessment information for more than just assigning grades to students. Instead, assessments of activities requiring students to actively engage in their learning, such as student journaling in STEM Research Notebooks, collaborative presentations, and constructing graphic organizers, should be used to move student learning forward. Whereas other curriculum with assessments may include

objective-type (multiple-choice or matching) tests, quizzes, or worksheets, we have intentionally avoided these forms of assessments to better align assessment strategies with teacher instruction and student learning techniques. Since the focus of this book is on project- or problem-based STEM curriculum and instruction that focuses on higher-level thinking skills, appropriate and authentic performance assessments were developed to elicit the most reliable and valid indication of growth in student abilities (Brookhart and Nitko 2008).

Comprehensive Assessment System

Assessment throughout all STEM Road Map curriculum modules acts as a comprehensive system in which formative and summative assessments work together to provide teachers with high-quality information on student learning. Formative assessment occurs when the teacher finds out formally or informally what a student knows about a smaller, defined concept or skill and provides timely feedback to the student about his or her level of proficiency. Summative assessments occur when students have performed all activities in the module and are given a cumulative performance evaluation in which they demonstrate their growth in learning.

A comprehensive assessment system can be thought of as akin to a sporting event. Formative assessments are the practices: It is important to accomplish them consistently, they provide feedback to help students improve their learning, and making mistakes can be worthwhile if students are given an opportunity to learn from them. Summative assessments are the competitions: Students need to be prepared to perform at the best of their ability. Without multiple opportunities to practice skills along the way through formative assessments, students will not have the best chance of demonstrating growth in abilities through summative assessments (Black and Wiliam 1998).

Embedded Formative Assessments

Formative assessments in this module serve two main purposes: to provide feedback to students about their learning and to provide important information for the teacher to inform immediate instructional needs. Providing feedback to students is particularly important when conducting problem- or project-based learning because students take on much of the responsibility for learning, and teachers must facilitate student learning in an informed way. For example, if students are required to conduct research for the Activity/Exploration phase but are not familiar with what constitutes a reliable resource, they may develop misconceptions based on poor information. When a teacher monitors this learning through formative assessments and provides specific feedback related to the instructional goals, students are less likely to develop incomplete or incorrect conceptions in their independent investigations. By using formative assessment to detect problems in student learning and then acting on this information, teachers help move student learning forward through these teachable moments.

Formative assessments come in a variety of formats. They can be informal, such as asking students probing questions related to student knowledge or tasks or simply observing students engaged in an activity to gather information about student skills. Formative assessments can also be formal, such as a written quiz or a laboratory practical.

Regardless of the type, three key steps must be completed when using formative assessments (Sondergeld, Bell, and Leusner 2010). First, the assessment is delivered to students so that teachers can collect data. Next, teachers analyze the data (student responses) to determine student strengths and areas that need additional support. Finally, teachers use the results from information collected to modify lessons and create learning environments that reinforce weak points in student learning. If student learning information is not used to modify instruction, the assessment cannot be considered formative in nature. Formative assessments can be about content, science process skills, or even learning skills. When a formative assessment focuses on content, it assesses student knowledge about the disciplinary core ideas from the *Next Generation Science Standards* (*NGSS*) or content objectives from *Common Core State Standards for Mathematics* (*CCSS Mathematics*) or *Common Core State Standards for English Language Arts* (*CCSS ELA*). Content-focused formative assessments ask students questions about declarative knowledge regarding the concepts they have been learning. Process skills formative assessments examine the extent to which a student can perform science and engineering practices from the *NGSS* or process objectives from *CCSS Mathematics* or *CCSS ELA*, such as constructing an argument. Learning skills can also be assessed formatively by asking students to reflect on the ways they learn best during a module and identify ways they could have learned more.

Assessment Maps

Assessment maps or blueprints can be used to ensure alignment between classroom instruction and assessment. If what students are learning in the classroom is not the same as the content on which they are assessed, the resultant judgment made on student learning will be invalid (Brookhart and Nitko 2008). Therefore, the issue of instruction and assessment alignment is critical. The assessment map for this book (found in Chapter 3) indicates by lesson whether the assessment should be completed as a group or on an individual basis, identifies the assessment as formative or summative in nature, and aligns the assessment with its corresponding learning objectives.

Note that the module includes far more formative assessments than summative assessments. This is done intentionally to provide students with multiple opportunities to practice their learning of new skills before completing a summative assessment. Note also that formative assessments are used to collect information on only one or two learning objectives at a time so that potential relearning or instructional modifications can focus on smaller and more manageable chunks of information. Conversely,

summative assessments in the module cover many more learning objectives, as they are traditionally used as final markers of student learning. This is not to say that information collected from summative assessments cannot or should not be used formatively. If teachers find that gaps in student learning persist after a summative assessment is completed, it is important to revisit these existing misconceptions or areas of weakness before moving on (Black et al. 2003).

SELF-REGULATED LEARNING THEORY IN THE STEM ROAD MAP MODULES

Many learning theories are compatible with the STEM Road Map modules, such as constructivism, situated cognition, and meaningful learning. However, we feel that the self-regulated learning theory (SRL) aligns most appropriately (Zimmerman 2000). SRL requires students to understand that thinking needs to be motivated and managed (Ritchhart, Church, and Morrison 2011). The STEM Road Map modules are student centered and are designed to provide students with choices, concrete hands-on experiences, and opportunities to see and make connections, especially across subjects (Eliason and Jenkins 2012; NAEYC 2016). Additionally, SRL is compatible with the modules because it fosters a learning environment that supports students' motivation, enables students to become aware of their own learning strategies, and requires reflection on learning while experiencing the module (Peters and Kitsantas 2010).

The theory behind SRL (see Figure 2.2) explains the different processes that students engage in before, during, and after a learning task. Because SRL is a cyclical learning process, the accomplishment of one cycle develops strategies for the next learning cycle. This cyclic way of learning aligns with the various sections in the STEM Road Map lesson plans on Introductory Activity/ Engagement, Activity/ Exploration, Explanation, Elaboration/Application of Knowledge, and Evaluation/Assessment. Since the students engaged in a module take on much of the responsibility for learning, this theory also provides guidance for teachers to keep students on the right track.

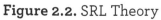

Figure 2.2. SRL Theory

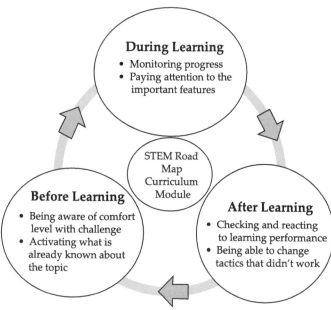

Source: Adapted from Zimmerman 2000.

Table 2.1. SRL Learning Process Components

Learning Process Components	Example from Mineral Resources Module	Lesson Number
Before Learning		
Motivates students	Students should be paired to brainstorm initial questions and responses related to this statement: *Individuals take for granted the availability of mineral resources.*	Lesson 1
Evokes prior learning	Student pairs generate a list of the everyday items they used before school. Students use the internet to research what minerals are common source materials for the elements used to make one of the items The teacher can choose one to discuss as exemplar.	Lesson 1
During Learning		
Focuses on important features	After receiving an overview of extraction methods, students do research to discover the mining process for their selected mineral from beginning to end, including how the mineral is mined, processed or refined once removed from the ground, any special handling procedures, and how that mineral is eventually used by consumers	Lesson 2
Helps students monitor their progress	Students must be able to explain why their device is better for the Earth and our society, but should also acknowledge any apparent disadvantages of their new device.	Lesson 2
After Learning		
Evaluates learning	Students will complete the culminating activity in this module – a website explaining the way minerals in an everyday object are mined and the potential impacts on the environment. The website will be evaluated by peers and the teacher.	Lesson 3
Takes account of what worked and what did not work	Students will write a reflection of the review of their challenge presentation of the website.	Lesson 3

The remainder of this section explains how SRL theory is embedded within the five sections of each module and points out ways to support students in becoming independent learners of STEM while productively functioning in collaborative teams.

Before Learning: Setting the Stage

Before attempting a learning task such as the STEM Road Map modules, teachers should develop an understanding of their students' level of comfort with the process of accomplishing the learning and determine what they already know about the topic. When students are comfortable with attempting a learning task, they tend to take more risks in learning and as a result achieve deeper learning (Bandura 1986).

The STEM Road Map curriculum modules are designed to foster excitement from the very beginning. Each module has an Introductory Activity/Engagement section that introduces the overall topic from a unique and exciting perspective, engaging the students to learn more so that they can accomplish the challenge. The Introductory Activity also has a design component that helps teachers assess what students already know about the topic of the module. In addition to the deliberate designs in the lesson plans to support SRL, teachers can support a high level of student comfort with the learning challenge by finding out if students have ever accomplished the same kind of task and, if so, asking them to share what worked well for them.

During Learning: Staying the Course

Some students fear inquiry learning because they aren't sure what to do to be successful (Peters 2010). However, the STEM Road Map curriculum modules are embedded with tools to help students pay attention to knowledge and skills that are important for the learning task and to check student understanding along the way. One of the most important processes for learning is the ability for learners to monitor their own progress while performing a learning task (Peters 2012). The modules allow students to monitor their progress with tools such as the STEM Research Notebooks, in which they record what they know and can check whether they have acquired a complete set of knowledge and skills. The STEM Road Map modules support inquiry strategies that include previewing, questioning, predicting, clarifying, observing, discussing, and journaling (Morrison and Milner 2014). Through the use of technology throughout the modules, inquiry is supported by providing students access to resources and data while enabling them to process information, report the findings, collaborate, and develop 21st century skills.

It is important for teachers to encourage students to have an open mind about alternative solutions and procedures (Milner and Sondergeld 2015) when working through the STEM Road Map curriculum modules. Novice learners can have difficulty knowing what to pay attention to and tend to treat each possible avenue for information as equal (Benner 1984). Teachers are the mentors in a classroom and can point out ways for students to approach learning during the Activity/Exploration, Explanation, and Elaboration/Application of Knowledge portions of the lesson plans to ensure that students pay attention to the important concepts and skills throughout the module. For example, if a student is to demonstrate conceptual awareness of motion when working on roller coaster research, but the student has misconceptions about motion, the teacher can step in and redirect student learning.

After Learning: Knowing What Works

The classroom is a busy place, and it may often seem that there is no time for self-reflection on learning. Although skipping this reflective process may save time in the short term, it reduces the ability to take into account things that worked well and things that didn't so that teaching the module may be improved next time. In the long run, SRL skills are critical for students to become independent learners who can adapt to new situations. By investing the time it takes to teach students SRL skills, teachers can save time later, because students will be able to apply methods and approaches for learning that they have found effective to new situations. In the Evaluation/Assessment portion of the STEM Road Map curriculum modules, as well as in the formative assessments throughout the modules, two processes in the after-learning phase are supported: evaluating one's own performance and accounting for ways to adapt tactics that didn't work well. Students have many opportunities to self-assess in formative assessments, both in groups and individually, using the rubrics provided in the modules.

The designs of the *NGSS* and *CCSS* allow for students to learn in diverse ways, and the STEM Road Map curriculum modules emphasize that students can use a variety of tactics to complete the learning process. For example, students can use STEM Research Notebooks to record what they have learned during the various research activities. Note- book entries might include putting objectives in students' own words, compiling their prior learning on the topic, documenting new learning, providing proof of what they learned, and reflecting on what they felt successful doing and what they felt they still needed to work on. Perhaps students didn't realize that they were supposed to connect what they already knew with what they learned. They could record this and would be prepared in the next learning task to begin connecting prior learning with new learning.

SAFETY IN STEM

Student safety is a primary consideration in all subjects but is an area of particular concern in science, where students may interact with unfamiliar tools and materials that may pose additional safety risks. It is important to implement safety practices within the context of STEM investigations, whether in a classroom laboratory or in the field. When you keep safety in mind as a teacher, you avoid many potential issues with the lesson while also protecting your students.

STEM safety practices encompass things considered in the typical science class-room. Ensure that students are familiar with basic safety considerations, such as wearing protective equipment (e.g., safety glasses or goggles and latex-free gloves) and taking care with sharp objects, and know emergency exit procedures. Teachers should learn beforehand the locations of the safety eyewash, fume hood, fire extinguishers, and emergency shut-off switch in the classroom and how to use them. Also be aware of any school or district safety policies that are in place and apply those that align with the work being conducted in the lesson. It is important to review all safety procedures annually.

STEM investigations should always be supervised. Each lesson in the modules includes teacher guidelines for applicable safety procedures that should be followed. Before each investigation, teachers should go over these safety procedures with the student teams. Some STEM focus areas such as engineering require that students can demonstrate how to properly use equipment in the maker space before the teacher allows them to proceed with the lesson.

Information about classroom science safety, including a safety checklist for science class- rooms, general lab safety recommendations, and links to other science safety resources, is available at the Council of State Science Supervisors (CSSS) website at *www.csss-science.org/safety.shtml*. The National Science Teaching Association (NSTA) provides a list of science rules and regulations, including standard operating procedures for lab safety, and a safety acknowledgment form for students and parents or guardians to sign. You can access these resources at *http://static.nsta.org/pdfs/SafetyIn-TheScienceClassroom.pdf*. In addition, NSTA's Safety in the Science Classroom web page (*www.nsta.org/safety*) has numerous links to safety resources, including papers written by the NSTA Safety Advisory Board.

Disclaimer: The safety precautions for each activity are based on use of the recommended materials and instructions, legal safety standards, and better professional practices. Using alternative materials or procedures for these activities may jeopardize the level of safety and therefore is at the user's own risk.

REFERENCES

Bandura, A. 1986. *Social foundations of thought and action: A social cognitive theory.* Englewood Cliffs, NJ: Prentice-Hall.

Barell, J. 2006. *Problem-based learning: An inquiry approach.* Thousand Oaks, CA: Corwin Press.

Benner, P. 1984. *From novice to expert: Excellence and power in clinical nursing practice.* Menlo Park, CA: Addison-Wesley Publishing Company.

Black, P., C. Harrison, C. Lee, B. Marshall, and D. Wiliam. 2003. *Assessment for learning: Putting it into practice.* Berkshire, UK: Open University Press.

Black, P., and D. Wiliam. 1998. Inside the black box: Raising standards through classroom assessment. *Phi Delta Kappan* 80 (2): 139–148.

Blumenfeld, P., E. Soloway, R. Marx, J. Krajcik, M. Guzdial, and A. Palincsar. 1991. Motivating project- based learning: Sustaining the doing, supporting learning. *Educational Psychologist* 26 (3): 369–398.

Brookhart, S. M., and A. J. Nitko. 2008. *Assessment and grading in classrooms.* Upper Saddle River, NJ: Pearson.

Bybee, R., J. Taylor, A. Gardner, P. Van Scotter, J. Carlson, A. Westbrook, and N. Landes. 2006. *The BSCS 5E instructional model: Origins and effectiveness. http://science.education.nih.gov/ houseofreps. nsf/b82d55fa138783c2852572c9004f5566/$FILE/Appendix?D.pdf.*

Eliason, C. F., and L. T. Jenkins. 2012. *A practical guide to early childhood curriculum.* 9th ed. New York: Merrill.

Johnson, C. 2003. Bioterrorism is real-world science: Inquiry-based simulation mirrors real life. *Science Scope* 27 (3): 19–23.

Krajcik, J., and P. Blumenfeld. 2006. Project-based learning. In *The Cambridge handbook of the learning sciences*, ed. R. Keith Sawyer, 317–334. New York: Cambridge University Press.

Lambros, A. 2004. *Problem-based learning in middle and high school classrooms: A teacher's guide to implementation.* Thousand Oaks, CA: Corwin Press.

Milner, A. R., and T. Sondergeld. 2015. Gifted urban middle school students: The inquiry continuum and the nature of science. *National Journal of Urban Education and Practice* 8 (3): 442–461.

Morrison, V., and A. R. Milner. 2014. Literacy in support of science: A closer look at cross-curricular instructional practice. *Michigan Reading Journal* 46 (2): 42–56.

National Association for the Education of Young Children (NAEYC). 2016. Developmentally appropriate practice position statements. *www.naeyc.org/positionstatements/dap.*

Peters, E. E. 2010. Shifting to a student-centered science classroom: An exploration of teacher and student changes in perceptions and practices. *Journal of Science Teacher Education* 21 (3): 329–349.

Peters, E. E. 2012. Developing content knowledge in students through explicit teaching of the nature of science: Influences of goal setting and self- monitoring. *Science and Education* 21 (6): 881–898.

Peters, E. E., and A. Kitsantas. 2010. The effect of nature of science metacognitive prompts on science students' content and nature of science knowledge, metacognition, and self-regulatory efficacy. *School Science and Mathematics* 110: 382–396.

Popham, W. J. 2013. *Classroom assessment: What teachers need to know.* 7th ed. Upper Saddle River, NJ: Pearson.

Ritchhart, R., M. Church, and K. Morrison. 2011. *Making thinking visible: How to promote engagement, understanding, and independence for all learners.* San Francisco, CA: Jossey-Bass.

Sondergeld, T. A., C. A. Bell, and D. M. Leusner. 2010. Understanding how teachers engage in formative assessment. *Teaching and Learning* 24 (2): 72–86.

Zimmerman, B. J. 2000. Attaining self-regulation: A social-cognitive perspective. In *Handbook of self-regulation*, ed. M. Boekaerts, P. Pintrich, and M. Zeidner, 13–39. San Diego: Academic Press.

PART 2

MINERAL RESOURCES
STEM ROAD MAP MODULE

MINERAL RESOURCES MODULE OVERVIEW

Erin E. Peters-Burton, Giuseppina Mattietti, Jennifer Drake Patrick, Brad Rankin, Anthony Pellegrino, Susan Poland, Janet B. Walton, and Carla C. Johnson

THEME: Optimizing the Human Experience

LEAD DISCIPLINES: Science and English/Language Arts

MODULE SUMMARY

A democratic society requires citizens to actively participate. The intention of this PBL module is to engage students in examining a controversial issue that affects society and make an informed decision. Through their work, students will develop an in depth understanding of mineral resources by researching the utility and impact of particular mineral resources on society. Students will then work in teams to locate quantitative and qualitative data on mineral resources and discern the reliability of the information. Students will use their data to write an opinion article to be published in an online newspaper and then develop a website to convince readers of the effectiveness of a particular design solution for developing, managing, and utilizing mineral resources. The purpose of this project is to build students' knowledge about mineral resources and challenge them to make an informed decision about a critical topic in society with the goal of encouraging students to become informed citizens who will contribute to the functioning of a democratic society (adapted from Peters-Burton, Seshaiyer, Burton, Drake-Patrick, and Johnson, 2015; see https://www.routledge.com/products/9781138804234).

ESTABLISHED GOALS/OBJECTIVES

A goal for this PBL module is for students to understand how researching an issue is important in making informed decisions. Students will be expected to demonstrate their understanding of mineral resources by preparing a compelling argument in an opinion article to inform the public about solutions for effectively managing and using mineral resources.

DOI: 10.4324/9781003261742-5

The objectives are as follows:

    a.   students will be able to explain where mineral resources are located and used in various ways in society.

    b.   students will be able to explain why mineral resources are important to society.

    c.   students will be able to critically evaluate quantitative and qualitative data about mineral resources.

    d.   students will be able to write an opinion article demonstrating their knowledge about competing design solutions for addressing one aspect related to mineral resources they found most compelling.

The Next Generation Science Standards (NGSS) crosscutting concepts in this module are cause and effect; systems and system models; and energy and matter. Students will examine how particular practices for locating and extracting mineral resources impact the environment and further analyze how the global demand for mineral resources drives the innovation of ideas for how to best manage, develop, and use mineral resources. Students will engage in science and engineering practices such as asking questions and defining problems, designing and using models, planning and carrying out investigations, analyzing and interpreting data, using mathematics and computational thinking, constructing explanations (for science) and designing solutions (for engineering), engaging in argument from evidence, and obtaining, evaluating, and communicating information by evaluating competing design solutions for developing, managing, and utilizing mineral resources based on cost-benefit ratios with both qualitative and quantitative criteria. Students will then communicate their learning through writing an opinion article to be published or through the development of a website with the assistance of software tools that presents evidence for the use of particular design solutions. Language objectives are met through the use of argumentation in science, social studies objectives are met through researching current and historical uses and practices of locating mineral resources as well as public policy on mineral resources, and mathematics objectives are met through analysis of qualitative and quantitative data and cost-benefit ratios.

Driving questions:

- How limited are the mineral resources that we currently use for technology?

- How much impact does extracting mineral resources from the Earth have on the environment?

- Could there be more environmentally friendly ways to extract mineral resources?

Who owns the valuable mineral resources in the Earth? People who own the property or the people who have the technology to extract them? How might disputes between these groups be settled?

CHALLENGE AND/OR PROBLEM FOR STUDENTS TO SOLVE

Designing a website for a global demand on minerals: Students will investigate the question "How does society meet the global demand for mineral resources?" Students will establish an understanding of the demand for mineral resources by examining the mineral components of everyday items and considering the impact of obtaining these mineral resources from the Earth. Students will explore how mineral resource are extracted, refined, and distributed for various use and applications. Furthermore, they will analyze the economic, environmental, and potential health impact of mining and develop an opinion article from their research. Students will then be challenged to work with a small group to collect and examine data on a particular mineral and draw conclusions about effective solutions for developing, managing, and using that mineral resource. Students will then develop a website to present their findings.

CONTENT STANDARDS ADDRESSED IN THIS STEM ROAD MAP MODULE

A full listing with descriptions of the standards this module addresses can be found in the appendix. Listings of the particular standards addressed within lessons are provided in a table for each lesson in Chapter 4.

STEM RESEARCH NOTEBOOK

Each student should maintain a STEM Research Notebook, which will serve as a place for students to organize their work throughout this module (see p. 12 for more general discussion on setup and use of the notebook). All written work in the module should be included in the notebook, including records of students' thoughts and ideas, fictional accounts based on the concepts in the module, and records of student progress through the EDP. The notebooks may be maintained across subject areas, giving students the opportunity to see that although their classes may be separated during the school day, the knowledge they gain is connected. You may also wish to have students include the STEM Research Notebook Guidelines student handout on page 29 in their notebooks.

Emphasize to students the importance of organizing all information in a Research Notebook. Explain to them that scientists and other researchers maintain detailed Research Notebooks in their work. These notebooks, which are crucial to researchers' work because they contain critical information and track the researchers' progress, are often considered legal documents for scientists who are pursuing patents or wish to provide proof of their discovery process.

STEM RESEARCH NOTEBOOK GUIDELINES

STEM professionals record their ideas, inventions, experiments, questions, observations, and other work details in notebooks so that they can use these notebooks to help them think about their projects and the problems they are trying to solve. You will each keep a STEM Research Notebook during this module that is like the notebooks that STEM professionals use. In this notebook, you will include all your work and notes about ideas you have. The notebook will help you connect your daily work with the big problem or challenge you are working to solve.

It is important that you organize your notebook entries under the following headings:

1. **Chapter Topic or Title of Problem or Challenge:** You will start a new chapter in your STEM Research Notebook for each new module. This heading is the topic or title of the big problem or challenge that your team is working to solve in this module.

2. **Date and Topic of Lesson Activity for the Day:** Each day, you will begin your daily entry by writing the date and the day's lesson topic at the top of a new page. Write the page number both on the page and in the table of contents.

3. **Information Gathered from Research:** This is information you find from outside resources such as websites or books.

4. **Information Gained from Class or Discussions with Team Members:** This information includes any notes you take in class and notes about things your team discusses. You can include drawings of your ideas here, too.

5. **New Data Collected from Investigations:** This includes data gathered from experiments, investigations, and activities in class.

6. **Documents:** These are handouts and other resources you may receive in class that will help you solve your big problem or challenge. Paste or staple these documents in your STEM Research Notebook for safekeeping and easy access later.

7. **Personal Reflections:** Here, you record your own thoughts and ideas on what you are learning.

8. **Lesson Prompts:** These are questions or statements that your teacher assigns you within each lesson to help you solve your big problem or challenge. You will respond to the prompts in your notebook.

9. **Other Items:** This section includes any other items your teacher gives you or other ideas or questions you may have.

MODULE LAUNCH

In the opening activity, students will examine their own knowledge about mineral resources in their everyday lives. This is a critical exercise because it is an opportunity for the teacher to diagnose any misconceptions to inform future lessons and access students' background knowledge about the topic. The teacher will post the following thought-provoking statement to engage students in purposeful exploration of the topic:

Individuals take for granted the availability of mineral resources.

A synopsis of this statement can be accessed through the USGS Mineral Resource Program website (USGS, 2009). This should access students' prior knowledge and build interest in the topic of mineral resources The teacher can then introduce the unit of study and encourage students to examine the questions generated through the initial activity as they continue to explore the global demands for mineral resources. Encourage students to pay attention to news headlines and other media outlets for information about topics related to societal use of mineral resources. Consider creating a board in the classroom or a virtual board where students can post links to current events connected to the ideas in this module.

PREREQUISITE SKILLS FOR THE MODULE

High school students have had experience with Earth science in elementary and middle school so they should have basic knowledge about mineral resources including what a mineral is, examples of minerals, and how they are extracted and used in society. The focus of this unit will move beyond that basic knowledge to develop a deeper understanding of how the global demand for mineral resources impacts society. Students should have some basic experience analyzing qualitative and quantitative data and locating and analyzing a variety of resources. Table 3.1 provides an overview of prerequisite skills and knowledge that students are expected to apply in this module, along with examples of how they apply this knowledge throughout the module. Differentiation strategies are also provided for students who may need additional support in acquiring or applying this knowledge.

Table 3.1. Prerequisite Key Knowledge and Examples of Differentiation

Prerequisite key knowledge	Application of knowledge	Differentiation for students needing knowledge
Minerals are formed in the Earth and have specific physical and chemical properties (i.e. hardness, cleavage, density, luster).	Students can identify common rock-forming minerals by their properties. Instructors might have a set of common minerals and rocks and testing kit available for demo.	Students needing support in this knowledge can review the physical properties of minerals by visiting. http://www.kidsloverocks.com/html/physical_properties_of_mineral.html http://www.mineralogy4kids.org/
Mineral resources are used in everyday living.	Students will explain how mineral resources s are used in everyday items.	Students needing support for this knowledge may benefit from a review with the teacher or being paired in a group with students who can share their knowledge. The teacher may also use media presentations in the resource list to further develop students' background knowledge as needed. A useful website is https://pubs.usgs.gov/of/2001/0360/
Minerals are extracted from the Earth's crust.	Students will be able to explain how mineral resources are extracted from the Earth.	Students needing support in this knowledge may benefit from a review of these concepts with the teacher. These links may be helpful on how mineral resources are extracted: (https://www.youtube.com/watch?v=GLFd4nnEAY4) https://www.youtube.com/watch?v=LI0Zh_7XUdw

POTENTIAL STEM MISCONCEPTIONS

Students enter the classroom with a wide variety of prior knowledge and ideas, so it is important to be alert to misconceptions, or inappropriate understandings of foundational knowledge. These misconceptions can be classified as one of several types: "preconceived notions," opinions based on popular beliefs or understandings; "nonscientific beliefs," knowledge students have gained about science from sources outside the scientific community; "conceptual misunderstandings," incorrect conceptual models based on incomplete understanding of concepts; "vernacular misconceptions," misunderstandings of words based on their common use versus their scientific use; and "factual misconceptions," incorrect or imprecise knowledge learned in early life that remains unchallenged (NRC 1997, p. 28). Misconceptions must be addressed and dismantled in order for students to reconstruct their knowledge, and therefore teachers should be prepared to take the following steps:

- *Identify students' misconceptions.*

- *Provide a forum for students to confront their misconceptions.*

- *Help students reconstruct and internalize their knowledge, based on scientific models.* (*NRC 1997, p. 29*)

Keeley and Harrington (2010) recommend using diagnostic tools such as probes and formative assessment to identify and confront student misconceptions and begin the process of reconstructing student knowledge. Keeley and Harrington's *Uncovering Student Ideas in Science* series contains probes targeted toward uncovering student misconceptions in a variety of areas. In particular, Volume 1 of *Uncovering Student Ideas in Earth and Environmental Science* (Tucker and Keeley 2016), about formative assessment probes, may be a useful resource for addressing student misconceptions in this module.

Some commonly held misconceptions specific to lesson content are provided with each lesson so that you can be alert for student misunderstanding of the science concepts presented and used during this module. The American Association for the Advancement of Science has also identified misconceptions that students frequently hold regarding various science concepts (see the links at *http://assessment.aaas.org/topics*).

Table 3.2. Sample STEM Misconceptions

Topic	Student Misconception	Explanation
Engineering Design Process (EDP)	Engineers only use the EDP to create physical items.	The EDP is used to create a solution to a problem. Ideas can be designed just as physical objects are.
Mineral resources	Minerals are used to make physical items.	Mineral resources is a definition that includes metallic resources, ore, and non-metallic resources, such as building stones, and energy resources like fossil fuels and nuclear fuel.
Mineral extraction: separating a mineral from the Earth's crust for production	Mineral resources are unimportant in today's industrial civilization.	Minerals are a key part of ubiquitous technologies such as cell phones and computers. Mining is a necessity to keep the supply equal to the demand for new technologies.
	Mineral extraction is environmentally devastating.	Each mining operation is a complex system that affects not only the natural environment but also the social and economic aspects of the world where it is found. It is a complex system and its effects can be seen in time well past its closure.
	Mineral resources are mined ready to be used.	A mineral resource needs to undergo several steps in refining before becoming available to make the object we need.

SRL PROCESS COMPONENTS

Table 3.3 illustrates some of the activities in the Rebuilding the Natural Environment module and how they align to the SRL process before, during, and after learning.

Table 3.3. SRL Process Components

Learning Process Components	Example from Mineral Resources Module	Lesson Number
Before Learning		
Motivates students	Students should be paired to brainstorm initial questions and responses related to this statement: *Individuals take for granted the availability of mineral resources.*	Lesson 1
Evokes prior learning	Student pairs generate a list of the everyday items they used before school. Students use the internet to research what minerals are common source materials for the elements used to make one of the items The teacher can choose one to discuss as exemplar.	Lesson 1
During Learning		
Focuses on important features	After receiving an overview of extraction methods, students do research to discover the mining process for their selected mineral from beginning to end, including how the mineral is mined, processed or refined once removed from the ground, any special handling procedures, and how that mineral is eventually used by consumers.	Lesson 2
Helps students monitor their progress	Students must be able to explain why their device is better for the Earth and our society, but should also acknowledge any apparent disadvantages of their new device.	Lesson 2
After Learning		
Evaluates learning	Students will complete the culminating activity in this module – a website explaining the way minerals in an everyday object are mined and the potential impacts on the environment. The website will be evaluated by peers and the teacher.	Lesson 3
Takes account of what worked and what did not work	Students will write a reflection of the review of their challenge presentation of the website.	Lesson 3

STRATEGIES FOR DIFFERENTIATING INSTRUCTION WITHIN THIS MODULE

For the purposes of this curriculum module, differentiated instruction is conceptualized as a way to tailor instruction including process, content, and product to various student needs in your class. A number of differentiation strategies are integrated into lessons across the module. The problem- and project-based learning approach used in the lessons is designed to address students' multiple intelligences by providing a variety of entry points and methods to investigate the key concepts in the module (for example, investigating minerals from the perspectives of science and social issues via scientific inquiry, literature, journaling, and collaborative design). Differentiation strategies for students needing support in prerequisite knowledge can be found in Table 3.1 (p. 29). You are encouraged to use information gained about student prior knowledge during introductory activities and discussions to inform your instructional differentiation. Strategies incorporated into this lesson include flexible grouping, varied environmental learning contexts, assessments, compacting, tiered assignments, and scaffolding

Flexible Grouping: Students have the opportunity to learn in various contexts throughout the module, including alone, in groups, in quiet reading and research-oriented activities, and in active learning through inquiry and design activities. In addition, students learn in a variety of ways, including through doing inquiry activities, journaling, reading texts, watching videos, participating in class discussion, and conducting web-based research.

Varied Environmental Learning Contexts: Students have the opportunity to learn in various contexts throughout the module, including alone, in groups, in quiet reading and research-oriented activities, and in active learning through inquiry and design activities. In addition, students learn in a variety of ways, including through doing inquiry activities, journaling, reading a variety of texts, watching videos, participating in class discussion, and conducting web-based research.

Assessments: Students are assessed in a variety of ways throughout the module, including individual and collaborative formative and summative assessments. Students have the opportunity to produce work via written text, oral and media presentations, and modeling. You may choose to provide students with additional choices of media for their products (for example, PowerPoint presentations, posters, or student-created websites or blogs).

Compacting: Based on student prior knowledge, you may wish to adjust instructional activities for students who exhibit prior mastery of a learning objective. You may wish to compile a classroom database of research resources and supplementary readings for a variety of reading levels and on a variety of topics related to the module's topic to provide opportunities for students to undertake independent reading.

Tiered Assignments and Scaffolding: Based on your awareness of student ability, understanding of concepts, and mastery of skills, you may wish to provide students with variations on activities by adding complexity to assignments or providing more or fewer learning supports for activities throughout the module. For instance, some students may need additional support in identifying key search words and phrases for web-based research or may benefit from cloze sentence handouts to enhance vocabulary understanding. Other students may benefit from expanded reading selections and additional reflective writing or from working with manipulatives and other visual representations of mathematical concepts. You may also work with your school librarian to compile a set of topical resources at a variety of reading levels.

STRATEGIES FOR ENGLISH LANGUAGE LEARNERS

Students who are developing proficiency in English language skills require additional supports to simultaneously learn academic content and the specialized language associated with specific content areas. WIDA has created a framework for providing support to these students and makes available rubrics and guidance on differentiating instructional materials for English language learners (ELLs) (see *www.wida.us/get. aspx?id=7*). In particular, ELL students may benefit from additional sensory supports such as images, physical modeling, and graphic representations of module content, as well as interactive support through collaborative work. This module incorporates a variety of sensory supports and provides ongoing opportunities for ELL students to work collaboratively.

Teachers differentiating instruction for ELL students should carefully consider the needs of these students as they introduce and use academic language in various language domains (listening, speaking, reading, and writing) throughout this module. To adequately differentiate instruction for ELL students, teachers should have an understanding of the proficiency level of each student. The following five overarching 9–12 WIDA learning standards are relevant to this module:

> Standard 1: Social and instructional language. Focus on social behavior in group work and class discussions.
>
> Standard 2: The language of language arts. Focus on forms of print, elements of text, picture books, comprehension strategies, main ideas and details, persuasive language, creating informational text, and editing and revising.
>
> Standard 3: The language of mathematics. Focus on numbers and operations, patterns, number sense, measurement, and strategies for problem solving.

Standard 4: The language of science. Focus on safety practices, energy sources, scientific process, and scientific inquiry.

Standard 5: The language of social studies. Focus on change from past to present, historical events, resources, transportation, map reading, and location of objects and places.

SAFETY CONSIDERATIONS FOR THE ACTIVITIES IN THIS MODULE

In this module, students create models variety of materials and should use caution when handling sharp objects and tools that can pinch. Students will also participate in investigations that involve electric current. Students should never touch any electrical equipment or circuits with wet hands and should never work with circuits near water. For more precautions, see the specific safety notes after the list of materials in each lesson. For more general safety guidelines, see the Safety in STEM section in Chapter 2 (p. 19).

DESIRED OUTCOMES AND MONITORING SUCCESS

The desired outcomes for this module are outlined in Table 3.4, along with suggested ways to gather evidence to monitor student success. For more specific details on desired outcomes, see the Established Goals and Objectives sections for the module and individual lessons.

Table 3.4. Desired Outcomes and Evidence of Success

Desired Outcome	Evidence of Success in Achieving Identified Outcome	
Students will explain how the demand for mineral resources impacts society and be able to use that knowledge to develop an opinion article and/or website that explains how and why particular design solutions are important.	Creating a poster to identify the cost/benefit analysis of using a particular mineral resource. Creating a device that converts one form of energy into another form of energy.	Communication of possible design solutions for developing, managing, and using mineral resources.

ASSESSMENT PLAN

Table 3.5 provides an overview of the major group and individual products and deliverables that comprise the assessment for this module. Table 3.6 provides a full assessment map of formative and summative assessments in this module.

Table 3.5. Major Products/Deliverables in Lead Disciplines – Group and Individual

Lesson	Major Group Products/Deliverables	Major Individual Products/Deliverables
1	Poster Presentation	STEM Research Notebooks Vocabulary knowledge charts Research question grid
2	Energy Device Rubric	STEM Research Notebooks Contribution to mineral study group project Cost-Benefit Analysis Chart
3	Mineral Website	STEM Research NotebooksOpinion Article

Table 3.6. Assessment Chart, Lead Disciplines – Mineral Resources

Lesson	Assessment	Group/Individual	Formative/Summative	Lesson Objective Assessed
1	STEM Research Notebook *prompts*	Group	Formative	Explain how mineral resources are used in everyday items.
1	Research Question *grid*	Group	Formative	Explain what make earth materials mineral resources and how mineral resources are refined.
1	Vocabulary Knowledge *chart*	Individual	Formative	Define and give examples of key vocabulary words.
1	Poster Presentation *rubric*	Group / Individual	Formative	Explain features of a specific mineral. Describe how a specific mineral is different from other minerals.
2	STEM Research Notebook *prompts*	Group / Individual	Formative	Explain mining and give examples of various types of mining. Compare and contrast extraction methods for obtaining minerals from the Earth.

Lesson	Assessment	Group/ Individual	Formative/ Summative	Lesson Objective Assessed
2	Cost-Benefit Analysis *chart*	Group	Formative	Analyze the costs and benefits of various mining techniques. Analyze and explain the environmental impact of mining. Discuss potential solutions for minimizing the impact on the environment. Calculate the cost-benefit ratios of design solutions for mineral resources.
2	Energy Device *rubric*	Group	Formative	Design a device for developing more sustainable practices for mining specific mineral resources.(i.e. copper for generators or silicon for photovoltaic cells).
3	STEM Research Notebook *prompts*	Group / Individual	Formative	Explain different perspectives on who owns mineral resources in Earth.
3	Website Production *rubric*	Group / Individual	Summative	Develop a website that informs readers about mineral resources. Advocate for certain position on mineral usage using references and research as support. Synthesize information from multiple sources. Use Engineering Design Process to create website. Present website.
3	Opinion Article *rubric*	Individual	Summative	Advocate for certain position on mineral usage using references and research as support. Synthesize information from multiple sources. Write cohesive article.

RESOURCES

School-based Individuals: Teachers can opt to co-teach portions of this unit and may want to combine classes for activities such as developing the opinion article and websites. The Media Specialist can help teachers locate resources for students to view and read about mineral resources. Special educators and reading specialists can help find supplemental sources for students needing extra support in reading and writing. Collaborating with the technology resource teacher for the website development could be helpful.

Technology: Internet access; tools for developing a website, tutorial for students.

Community: Guest speaker on mineral resources. Platforms for publishing opinion articles (newspapers, blogs, magazines, etc.).

Materials: Internet resources; library materials; a set of minerals and rock with testing kit.

MODULE TIMELINE

Tables 3.7–3.11 (pp. 40–42) provide lesson timelines for each week of the module. These timelines are provided for general guidance only and are based on class times of approximately 45 minutes.

Table 3.7. STEM Road Map Module Schedule Week One

Day 1	Day 2	Day 3	Day 4	Day 5
Lesson 1 *What is the global demand for mineral resources?* Students will respond to the thought-provoking statement and read an article about mineral resources to guide their investigation of mineral resources. Product: Set up STEM Research notebooks.	*Lesson 1* *What is the global demand for mineral resources?* Students will complete a Webquest using the USGS website to develop their understanding about the Mineral Resource Program and how to use this site to find reliable research. Product: Students should continue to generate a list of research questions about mineral resources and develop their research question grid.	*Lesson 1* *What is the global demand for mineral resources?* Students will meet in teams to conduct an Internet Search to find information about particular minerals and their uses. The Mineral Database (at https://www.mineralseducationcoalition.org/minerals) can guide students search. Student teams will select one mineral to investigate more deeply. Product: Students will begin to maintain their vocabulary knowledge charts.	*Lesson 1* *What is the global demand for mineral resources?* Student teams will continue to examine the potential use of and impact of that mineral resource. Product: Continue to fill in the Research Question Grid.	*Lesson 1* *What is the global demand for mineral resources?* Students will develop a poster presentation about their mineral. Class will brainstorm what should be included on posters.

Table 3.8. STEM Road Map Module Schedule Week Two

Day 6	Day 7	Day 8	Day 9	Day 10
Lesson 1	*Lesson 2*	*Lesson 2*	*Lesson 2*	*Lesson 2*
What is the global demand for mineral resources? Students will do a gallery walk of their posters, placing sticky notes with comments and questions on the posters. Product: Generate critical vocabulary list and next steps research questions.	*The Impact on Society* Students will watch _Ground Rules: Mining rights for a sustainable future_ and consider the social responsibility of mining through a fishbowl discussion. Product: Students should use a note-taking strategy and record ideas and reactions in their STEM Research notebooks.	*The Impact on Society* Students will continue to explore both qualitative and quantitative research on their mineral, with an emphasis now on understanding how it is mined and produced, and how that process impacts the Earth.	*The Impact on Society* Students will continue their reading and research. Groups should be discussing and formulating opinions about their work.	*The Impact on Society* Students will formulate a cost-benefit analysis for the production, consumption, and utilization of their mineral. Product: Cost-Benefit table.

Table 3.9. STEM Road Map Module Schedule Week Three

Day 11	Day 12	Day 13	Day 14	Day 15
Lesson 2	*Lesson 2*	*Lesson 2*	*Lesson 2*	*Lesson 2*
The Impact on Society Students will compare and contrast extraction methods for obtaining mineral resources from the Earth. Students will begin drafting an opinion article.	*The Impact on Society* Students will make a plan and begin creating a device or process to extract mineral resources that is more geo-friendly.	*The Impact on Society* Students will complete their device and develop a 3–5 minute explanation for their presentation.	*The Impact on Society* Students will present their devices and provide peer feedback.	*The Impact on Society* Students will review their feedback and draw final conclusions about their solution designs for their mineral resource.

Table 3.10. STEM Road Map Module Schedule Week Four

Day 16 Lesson Three	Day 17 Lesson Three	Day 18 Lesson Three	Day 19 Lesson Three	Day 20 Lesson Three
Lesson 2 The Impact on Society Students will choose an outlet for their opinion article and participate in peer review to finalize their articles for publication.	*Lesson 3* Why should citizens understand mineral use? Students will develop a timeline for creating their website and begin pre-production planning (coding, writing, materials needed, content, etc.)	*Lesson 3* Why should citizens understand mineral use? Students will engage in pre-production design.	*Lesson 3* Why should citizens understand mineral use? Create website	*Lesson 3* Why should citizens understand mineral use? Create website.

Table 3.11. STEM Road Map Module Schedule Week Five

Day 21 Lesson Three	Day 22 Lesson Three	Day 23 Lesson Three	Day 24 Lesson Three	Day 25 Lesson Three
Lesson 3 Why should citizens understand mineral use? Work on layout and design of websites.	*Lesson 3* Why should citizens understand mineral use? Work on websites.	*Lesson 3* Why should citizens understand mineral use? Finalize websites.	*Lesson 3* Why should citizens understand mineral use? Peer Review websites.	*Lesson 3* Why should citizens understand mineral use? Presentation of websites.

RESOURCES

Teachers have the option to co-teach portions of this module and may want to combine classes for activities such as developing websites. Computer science teachers can help students develop graphic images or animations, and art teachers can help students create three-dimensional models of minerals and their associated products. The media specialist can help teachers locate resources for students to view and read about minerals and mineral production and issues surrounding the need to meet society's mineral needs. Special educators and reading specialists can help find supplemental sources for students needing extra support in reading and writing. Additional resources may be found online. Community resources for this module may include guest speakers who work in energy production and electrical engineering, and those involved in resource conservation efforts related to energy.

REFERENCES

Keeley, P. and R. Harrington. 2010. *Uncovering student ideas in physical science, volume 1: 45 new force and motion assessment probes.* Arlington, VA: NSTA Press.

National Center for O*NET Development. Find Occupations. Retrieved from https://www.onetonline.org/find/

Peters-Burton, E. E., P. Seshaiyer, S. R. Burton, J. Drake-Patrick, and C. C. Johnson. 2015. The STEM Road Map for grades 9–12. In *STEM Road Map: A framework for integrated STEM education*, ed. C. C. Johnson, E. E. Peters-Burton, and T. J. Moore, 124–62. New York: Routledge. *www.routledge.com/products/9781138804234.*

WIDA Consortium. 2012. 2012 Amplification of the English language development standards: Kindergarten–grade 12. https://wida.wisc.edu

MINERAL RESOURCES LESSON PLANS

Erin E. Peters-Burton, Giuseppina Mattietti, Jennifer Drake-Patrick, Brad Rankin, Anthony Pellegrino, Susan Poland, Janet B. Walton, and Carla C. Johnson

Lesson Plan 1: Mineral Resources: What is the global demand for mineral resources?

LESSON ONE SUMMARY

Students will develop an understanding of how mineral resources are essential to society.

ESSENTIAL QUESTION(S)

How are mineral resources used in everyday living?

   What did you use today that was constructed of minerals?

   Why are minerals important to society?

   How are mineral resources discovered?

   Where are minerals found?

ESTABLISHED GOALS/OBJECTIVES

At the conclusion of this lesson, students will be able to:

- Explain how mineral resources are used in everyday items.

- Explain what are the steps from finding mineral resources to their utilization for everyday items.

- Compare the demand for mineral resources across the world.

TIME REQUIRED

6 days (approximately 45 minutes per day; Days 1–6 in schedule)

DOI: 10.4324/9781003261742-6

NECESSARY MATERIALS

Computer access to Internet for research.

Hand samples of mineral ore. If feasible, a visit to a local natural history museum or a rock gems and mineral show is highly recommended.

Hand samples of rocks and mineral ore.

Table 4.1. Content Standards Addressed in STEM Road Map Module Lesson One

NEXT GENERATION SCIENCE STANDARDS

PERFORMANCE EXPECTATIONS

HS-ETS1–1 Analyze a major global challenge to specify qualitative and quantitative criteria and constraints for solutions that account for societal needs and wants.

DISCIPLINARY CORE IDEAS

ETS1.A: Defining and Delimiting an Engineering Problem

Criteria and constraints also include satisfying any requirements set by society, such as taking issues of risk mitigation into account, and they should be quantified to the extent possible and stated in such a way that one can tell if a given design meets them. (secondary)

Humanity faces major global challenges today, such as the need for supplies of clean water and food or for energy sources that minimize pollution, which can be addressed through engineering. These global challenges also may have manifestations in local communities.

CROSSCUTTING CONCEPTS.

Connections to Engineering Technology, and Applications of Science

Influence of Science, Engineering and Technology on Society and the Natural World

Modern civilization depends on major technological systems. Engineers continuously modify these technological systems by applying scientific knowledge and engineering design practices to increase benefits while decreasing costs and risks.

Engineers continuously modify these technological systems by applying scientific knowledge and engineering design practices to increase benefits while decreasing costs and risks.

Analysis of costs and benefits is a critical aspect of decisions about technology.

SCIENCE AND ENGINEERING PRACTICES

Asking Questions and Defining Problems

Asking questions and defining problems in 9–12 builds on K–8 experiences and progresses to formulating, refining, and evaluating empirically testable questions and design problems using models and simulations.

Analyze complex real-world problems by specifying criteria and constraints for successful solutions.

COMMON CORE MATHEMATICS STANDARDS
MATHEMATICS PRACTICES

MP1 Make sense of problems and persevere in solving them.

MP2 Reason abstractly and quantitatively.

MP3 Construct viable arguments and critique the reasoning of others.

MP4 Model with mathematics.

MP5 Use appropriate tools strategically.

MP6 Attend to precision.

MATHEMATICS CONTENT

REI.D.11 Represent and solve equations and inequalities graphically.

COMMON CORE ENGLISH/LANGUAGE ARTS STANDARDS
READING STANDARDS

R111–12.1 Cite strong and thorough textual evidence to support analysis of what the text says explicitly as well as inferences drawn from the text, including determining where the text leaves matters uncertain.

R111–12.2 Determine two or more central ideas of a text and analyze their development over the course of the text, including how they interact and build on one another to provide a complex analysis; provide an objective summary of the text.

R111–12.3 Analyze a complex set of ideas or sequence of events and explain how specific individuals, ideas, or events interact and develop over the course of the text.

R111–12.4 Determine the meaning of words and phrases as they are used in a text, including figurative, connotative, and technical meanings; analyze how an author uses and refines the meaning of a key term or terms over the course of a text (e.g., how Madison defines faction in Federalist No. 10).

R111–12.6 Determine an author's point of view or purpose in a text in which the rhetoric is particularly effective, analyzing how style and content contribute to the power, persuasiveness or beauty of the text.

R111–12.8 Delineate and evaluate the reasoning in seminal U.S. texts, including the application of constitutional principles and use of legal reasoning (e.g., in U.S. Supreme Court majority opinions and dissents) and the premises, purposes, and arguments in works of public advocacy (e.g., The Federalist, presidential addresses).

R111–12.10 By the end of grade 11, read and comprehend literary nonfiction in the grades 11-CCR text complexity band proficiently, with scaffolding as needed at the high end of the range.

WRITING STANDARDS

W11–12.1a Introduce precise, knowledgeable claim(s), establish the significance of the claim(s), distinguish the claim(s) from alternate or opposing claims, and create an organization that logically sequences claim(s), counterclaims, reasons, and evidence.

Continued

Table 4.1. (*continued*)

W11–12.1b Develop claim(s) and counterclaims fairly and thoroughly, supplying the most relevant evidence for each while pointing out the strengths and limitations of both in a manner that anticipates the audience's knowledge level, concerns, values, and possible biases.

W11–12.1c Use words, phrases, and clauses as well as varied syntax to link the major sections of the text, create cohesion, and clarify the relationships between claim(s) and reasons, between reasons and evidence, and between claim(s) and counterclaims.

W11–12.1d Establish and maintain a formal style and objective tone while attending to the norms and conventions of the discipline in which they are writing.

W11–12.1e Provide a concluding statement or section that follows from and supports the argument presented.

W11–12.2a Introduce a topic; organize complex ideas, concepts, and information so that each new element builds on that which precedes it to create a unified whole; include formatting (e.g., headings), graphics (e.g., figures, tables), and multimedia when useful to aiding comprehension.

W11–12.2b Develop the topic thoroughly by selecting the most significant and relevant facts, extended definitions, concrete details, quotations, or other information and examples appropriate to the audience's knowledge of the topic.

W11–12.2c Use appropriate and varied transitions and syntax to link the major sections of the text, create cohesion, and clarify the relationships among complex ideas and concepts.

W11–12.2d Use precise language, domain-specific vocabulary, and techniques such as metaphor, simile, and analogy to manage the complexity of the topic.

W11–12.2e Establish and maintain a formal style and objective tone while attending to the norms and conventions of the discipline in which they are writing.

W11–12.2f Provide a concluding statement or section that follows from and supports the information or explanation presented (e.g., articulating implications or the significance of the topic).

W.11–12.4 Produce clear and coherent writing in which the development, organization, and style are appropriate to task, purpose, and audience.

W.11–12.5 Develop and strengthen writing as needed by planning, revising, editing, rewriting, or trying a new approach, focusing on addressing what is most significant for a specific purpose and audience.

W.11–12.8 Gather relevant information from multiple authoritative print and digital sources, using advanced searches effectively; assess the strengths and limitations of each source in terms of the task, purpose, and audience; integrate information into the text selectively to maintain the flow of ideas, avoiding plagiarism and overreliance on any one source and following a standard format for citation.

SPEAKING AND LISTENING STANDARDS

SL.11–12.1a Come to discussions prepared, having read and researched material under study; explicitly draw on that preparation by referring to evidence from texts and other research on the topic or issue to stimulate a thoughtful, well-reasoned exchange of ideas.

SL.11–12.1b Work with peers to promote civil, democratic discussions and decision-making, set clear goals and deadlines, and establish individual roles as needed.

SL.11–12.2 Integrate multiple sources of information presented in diverse formats and media (e.g., visually, quantitatively, orally) in order to make informed decisions and solve problems, evaluating the credibility and accuracy of each source and noting any discrepancies among the data.

SL.11–12.4 Present information, findings, and supporting evidence, conveying a clear and distinct perspective, such that listeners can follow the line of reasoning, alternative or opposing perspectives are addressed, and the organization, development, substance, and style are appropriate to purpose, audience, and a range of formal and informal tasks.

LITERACY STANDARDS

L.11–12.1a Apply the understanding that usage is a matter of convention, can change over time, and is sometimes contested.

L.11–12.1b Resolve issues of complex or contested usage, consulting references (e.g., Merriam-Webster's Dictionary of English Usage, Garner's Modern American Usage) as needed.

L.11–12.2 Demonstrate command of the conventions of standard English capitalization, punctuation, and spelling when writing.

L.11–12.2a Observe hyphenation conventions.

L.11–12.2a Spell correctly.

L.11–12.3a Vary syntax for effect, consulting references

L.11–12.6 Acquire and use accurately general academic and domain-specific words and phrases, sufficient for reading, writing, speaking, and listening at the college and career readiness level; demonstrate independence in gathering vocabulary knowledge when considering a word or phrase important to comprehension or expression.

21ST CENTURY SKILLS

Creativity and Innovation, Critical Thinking and Problem Solving, Communication and Collaboration, Information Literacy, Media Literacy, ICT Literacy, Flexibility and Adaptability, Initiative and Self-Direction, Social and Cross Cultural Skills, Productivity and Accountability, Leadership and Responsibility

Table 4.2. Key Vocabulary in Lesson One

Key Vocabulary*	Definition
Atom	The smallest particle of matter.
Compound	Matter that is composed of two or more types of elements.
Consumption	The utilization of goods and services to satisfy needs. Users are referred to as "consumers".

Continued

Table 4.2. (*continued*)

Key Vocabulary*	Definition
Element	A substance that is composed of a single type of atom.
Energy	Power derived from physical or chemical sources.
Extraction	The process of obtaining minerals from the Earth's crust.
Inorganic	Branch of chemistry dealing with compounds that are not made primarily of carbon; these compounds are associated with non-living things.
Mineral	A naturally occurring substance composed of one or more elements; has specific physical properties derived from its crystalline structure and its chemical composition.
Mining	The process of extracting resources including minerals from the Earth.
Mineral resource	Mineral resources are useful earth materials, like rocks, minerals, fossils and nuclear fuels, that are found in concentrations high enough that they can be mined for a profit.
Non-renewable resource	A resource that occurs in finite quantities such as coal.
Organic	Branch of chemistry dealing with compounds composed of carbon in combination with other elements; these compounds are associated with living things.
Production	The process or action of making goods and services from tangible (e.g. minerals, raw materials) and intangible (e.g. ideas, knowledge) resources. Factors including land, labor, capital, and entrepreneurship influence production.
Renewable resource	Natural resources that can be regenerated or replaced on a relevant timescale. Mineral resources, the result of the rock cycle, as non-renewable
Rock	A naturally occurring solid substance that is often composed of one or more minerals.

* Vocabulary terms are provided for both teacher and student use. Teachers may choose to introduce all or some terms to students.

TEACHER BACKGROUND INFORMATION

Teachers should have an understanding of what is meant by mineral resources, with an emphasis on understanding how they are essential to society. There are several free online resources that can provide updated information on the subject. For example, there are a variety of mineral resources that provide the necessary chemical elements used in mobile cell phones. Minerals such as Quartz provides Silicon, an element used both in the display and in the integrated circuitry of the device. A handout from the U.S. Department of Interior and the U.S. Geological Survey titled "a world of minerals in your mobile device" can be found here: https://pubs.usgs.gov/gip/0167/gip167.pdf.

Teachers should have knowledge of the data available from the USGS website (http://minerals.usgs.gov). There are many data sets that are freely available on this website. The following comprises a short list of the types of data sets found on the USGS website.

Name of Data Set	Brief description
Mineral Resources Data System	Describes deposit name, location, commodity, and references
Alaska Resource Data File	Describes mines, prospects, and mineral occurrences in Alaska
Global distribution of selected mines, deposits and districts of critical minerals	Approximate locations and descriptions of mines, deposits, and districts where critical minerals are found
Global assessment of undiscovered copper resources	Deposits, prospects, and permissive tracts for sediment-hosted copper resources world-wide
Volcanic massive sulfide deposits	Grade and tonnage models for all three subtypes of volcanic massive sulfide deposits and data allowing locations of all deposits to be plotted on GIS
Rare earth element mines, deposits, and occurrences	Location, geologic, and mineral economic data for world rare earth mines, deposits, and occurrences – coordinates for most of the deposits are available

This introductory lesson has a heavy vocabulary load so it is important to have strategies prepared for students who may need additional support (see http://www.adlit.org/article/c138/ for scores of strategies to build vocabulary such as Explicit Vocabulary Instruction, Developing "Student-Owned" Vocabulary, Cross Disciplinary Vocabulary Approach).

LESSON PREPARATION

Throughout this unit, students will maintain a STEM Research notebook. Teachers should prepare students to have a notebook on the first day. Teachers should explain

to students that all of their work will culminate in the production of a website and written article about their learning; therefore students should use their notebooks to record new information and write down reactions, questions, and analysis of their ideas (including pictures, concept maps, resource locations, etc.). Teachers should encourage students to use their STEM Research notebooks every day and leave time at the end of each class period for students to review their daily work and record new information in their notebooks (see this article about using and assessing science notebooks: https://www.nsta.org/publications/news/story.aspx?id=51882).

Teachers can emphasize the nature of science in this phase of the learning by emphasizing how the use of mineral resources has evolved over time, but that new research and data continues to inform public knowledge about how mineral resources can be better developed and managed with sustainable practices.

LEARNING PLAN COMPONENTS
Introductory Activity/Engagement

Connections to the Challenge: Begin each day of this lesson by directing students' attention to the driving question for the module and challenge, asking "How are mineral resources used in my life?" or "Why are mineral resources essential to society?" Hold a brief student discussion of how their learning in the previous days' lesson contributed to their ability to create their innovation for the final challenge. You may wish to hold a class discussion, creating a class list of key ideas on chart paper or the board, or you may wish to have students create a STEM Research Notebook entry with this information.

Science Class

Students will work in pairs to discuss the thought-provoking statement presented below.

STEM Research Notebook Prompt

Individuals take for granted the availability of mineral resources.

Students should be paired to brainstorm initial questions and responses related to this statement. Students should record their ideas in their STEM Research Notebooks in pairs, then the teacher should lead a discussion in which students share their ideas. Students should be encouraged to challenge one another's ideas in the discussion. Students should back up their statements with evidence when possible (though opinions should not be dismissed, given that this is an opinion statement).

After a few minutes, ask pairs to generate a list of the everyday items they used before school. Probe them to be specific (mobile phone, microwave, silverware, toothpaste, dog food, car, bus, etc.). Then, invite students to use the Internet to research what minerals are used to make one of the items. The teacher can choose one to model.

This very simple website, Mineralogy4Kids, has a tool where you can click on every-day items and a list of minerals in these items appear (http://www.mineralogy4kids.org/minerals-your-house). Further, teachers can click on the name of the material on this site to identify the formula, hardness, color, steak color, crystal system, and group of the mineral along with a short description and pictures of different configurations.

The teacher should elicit input from each pair and write contributions on the board. The teacher can note the minerals that are used multiple times in various items. Once this list is generated, the teacher can draw students back to the thought-provoking statement and gather data to test their opinion statements. Students should locate the website https://mrdata.usgs.gov/major-deposits/map-us.html (USGS Major mineral deposits of the world) and click on the icons on the map. Clicking on one of the shape icons on the map creates a sidebar that explains the record ID, name of the location, and type of mineral found there. If students click on the record ID, they will get details from the USGS about the location (Country, state or province, and longitude and lati-tude), type of mineral resource, also called commodity, deposit model, geologic map unit, and other scientific data near this location. Students can look broadly across the map to find locations that have rich mineral deposits and those that have sparse min-eral deposits. Cue students to connect the use of minerals with where they might be located in the world and if they take the use of that mineral for granted (or are not aware of how far that mineral had to be transported to get to their current location). Possibilities include political unrest in the area, expense to transport or limited supply of the mineral resource.

Teachers encourage students to think about their newly acquired knowledge of min-eral resources and formulate questions. Students might wonder: How do ores form? How do we refine an ore? How does a pollutant from a mine move through water, air, or sediment environments? The teacher can then lead a discussion, generating a list of recurring questions, topics, and ideas that can be used to guide subsequent lessons in the unit. Questions that students find particularly interesting can be noted on the Research Question Grid provided at the end of this lesson. This form can also be used as a brainstorming technique.

Mathematics Connections

Teachers have students identify the minerals used in a cell phone (they can use the USGS handout discussed in the science portion of this lesson or ask students to con-duct an Internet search) and the percentage of those minerals the U.S. imports. This resource from the Minerals Education Coalition provides a PDF of cell phone min-erals, the percentage of the mineral imported into the United States, and the major sources of the mineral: https://mineralseducationcoalition.org/wp-content/uploads/10_9_13cellphone.pdf.

Using a map of the world found at the end of this lesson, students will place different colored bubbles, each representing one of the minerals, on the countries from which the U.S. imports those minerals. The size of the bubbles will be proportional to the percentage of the mineral(s) imported from that country. Remind students to create a key of the colors and minerals those colors represent. Students will be asked to discuss the mineral contribution the U.S. makes towards its cell phone production. For ideas on using bubbles, see www.gapminder.org.

ELA Connections

Students will read the article *Do we take minerals for granted?* from the U.S. Geological Survey website (https://www.usgs.gov/programs/mineral-resources-program/do-we-take-minerals-granted). Invite students to read the bold headings and predict what they will learn about in this article. Students should write their predictions in their STEM Research Notebooks. Students should discuss their predictions in groups of four students and explain their rationale for making the prediction about the heading and reading. Students should then read the article to "test" their predictions. After the group of four students are finished reading their article, have them first discuss their prediction and then have a discussion summarizing the article. Students should record the summary of the article in their STEM Research Notebooks.

Teachers may want to use the Directed-Reading-Thinking Activity (DRTA) to support student comprehension of the assigned text (see http://www.nea.org/tools/directed-reading-thinking-activity.html.

Social Studies Connections

Begin by asking students to discuss why the U.S. Government establishes organizations such as the United States Geological Survey (USGS). Students can research how the United States Geological Survey (USGS) was established in 1879 and discuss its impact on the development and use of mineral resources (https://archive.usgs.gov/archive/sites/ar.water.usgs.gov/origin.html).

Place students into pairs and have them construct a verbal argument to support reasons why the USGS should continue to be funded by the U.S. Government. Student pairs should then meet with other student pairs to critique each other's argument. Students should construct a claim, back it up with evidence that they have accumulated from their ideas and from Internet searches, and construct reasons that the evidence supports the argument. A graphic organizer that can help students organize their ideas is found at the end of this lesson. A rubric to help students conduct a verbal argument and to help teachers assess verbal arguments is found at the end of this lesson. If there is time, have students brainstorm other federal agencies that they know about such as

NASA and the EPA. Have students research the origin of these agencies and discuss with the class.

ACTIVITY/INVESTIGATION
Science Class

Teachers should introduce the Mineral Data Base (https://www.mineralseducation coalition.org/minerals) and help students learn to use the tools in the database. Teachers should help students identify the features, properties, uses, and extraction methods for various minerals. Students will then get into pairs and choose a mineral to explore for their mineral study project. Students will use the information from their research to develop a poster to present their mineral.

Students should create their poster presentations according to the rubric at the end of this lesson.

Features of the posters include:

Content Knowledge	Demonstrates an exemplary understanding of the content presented.
Accuracy	All information is accurate and relevant.
Organization	Information is highly organized and presented in a logical manner.
Readability	Exemplary attendance to spelling, grammar, and punctuation; no or very few mistakes.

Students should pay particular attention to the quantitative and qualitative data that helps scientists understand the properties of the mineral, and how this data is used to set this mineral apart from others. Students should discuss the specific features that define the mineral in terms of its chemical composition and crystal formula and their mineral properties (like cleavage, hardness, streak, color, luster, solubility in HCl, and magnetism); should the students have sample of the minerals they choose, they will be able to perform the classical tests for mineral identification based on physical properties. This might not be possible for most economic minerals, in which the element concentration is highly dispersed in gangue (e.g. Bauxite for Aluminum). Depending on the choice of the mineral and the available resource, students might be able to design an original investigation of their mineral of choice (e.g. changes may be observed when exposed to ranges of temperature, diverse light wavelengths, etc.). In the posters, students will also illustrate the minerals extraction methods and their uses throughout history and in modern times. At the end of this assignment, students will hang their posters for their peers to evaluate on day six of the module.

Mathematics Connections

Students research the 40 most commonly used minerals and the percentage of those that the U.S. imports and exports. The USGS websites that were used earlier in this lesson can be a resource for this assignment. Students can also perform Internet searches for the lists of most commonly used minerals. Students will be tasked with determining the overall bulk mineral exports of the U.S. in relation to its imports. For example, if the U.S. exports 10,000 units of minerals and imports 100,000 units, then there is a 90,000-unit difference in favor of imports. Students should work in groups of 3 to create an infographic with the following information:

- The 40 most commonly used minerals

- Bulk units of export from the U.S.

- Bulk units of imports into the U.S.

- Result of the combinations of imports and exports (which direction is the difference?)

Students should perform a gallery walk of the infographics and take notes in their STEM Research Notebook about the posters that communicate the information most effectively. Hold a classroom wrap up discussion about the overall balance of imports and exports of minerals and the common features of the most effective ways of communicating these types of data. Students can improve their posters from science class based on the ideas that emerge from the infographics.

ELA Connections

Students will generate questions by participating in a Webquest on the USGS website (http://minerals.usgs.gov) to discover the purpose of the Mineral Resource Program and the resources available to them to learn more about minerals. According to the USGS website, The USGS Mineral Resources Program delivers unbiased science and information to understand mineral resource potential, production, consumption, and how minerals interact with the environment. Students should investigate their chosen mineral on this website and record important information in their STEM Research Notebook. Students should begin to generate specific questions to guide their research about the utility and impact of the mineral they are investigating for their mineral study group. Students can use the following strategies to help them generate questions about their mineral:

- Self-monitoring – What should I be looking for as I read?

- Collecting information – What are the facts about my mineral?

- Classifying – How can I organize this information to explain it clearly?

- Predicting – What might I want to know about how my mineral is produced, mined, used in everyday items, disposed of?

- See http://www.adlit.org/strategies/22093/ for ideas on helping students to generate purposeful questions to guide comprehension.

Social Studies Connections

Students can look at the trends in data across time for the demand and how particular minerals have been used in society (http://minerals.usgs.gov/minerals/).

On this website, students can go to Domestic Mineral Statistics by Commodity and click on their chosen mineral. Care should be taken into understanding that most chemical elements do not make their own minerals. For example, if a student chooses cadmium, which is a chemical element borne by zinc ore, by clicking on cadmium they will gain access to a refined mineral commodity summary, which might include import statistics, the value of mineral production, the rank of value, and the percent of U.S. total production by state. Students also have access to similar production statistics annually from 2013 to 2020, which they can graph to determine trends. The remainder of the summary report provides details for specific minerals about world reserves and resources. Students also have access on this page for older reports from 1998 to 2019.

Students should record the relevant statistics tables and trends in their STEM Research Notebook for their upcoming poster.

EXPLAIN
Science Class

Teachers will review and discuss the vocabulary knowledge chart, being sure to add in any critical vocabulary students will need to deepen their understanding. Students should clarify differences between rocks and minerals as critical to understand the steps to extraction of a certain mineral resource. Students will reason on the fact that a mineral resource is not usable as it is extracted, but it must undergo the process of refining, which is separating the needed chemical element/compound from the rock/mineral that has been extracted.

The teacher can give an example about the way gold is found: for gold nuggets found in placer deposits (streams), the refining has taken place through the long time it took for surface processes of erosion, transport, and deposition to accumulate the resource in the lowest energy setting of a stream. When gold is extracted from a mine, instead, the process of separating it from its ore requires a set of steps known in the industry as refining. Conceptually the process of refining is simple, it is a matter of triggering the right reaction in a controlled environment to separate the resource from its gangue. Human have been refining metals since the bronze age. For this science

class students can replicate the simple process of isolating a metal from its source rock in a similar way as people would have done in prehistoric times. The process for copper is relatively simple and can be done with few resources, provided a safe environment to carry out the experiment can be set up.

A classroom experiment to separate copper from copper ore can be carried out in as little as 1 hour, including setting up and time to make considerations and observations before and after. The choice to have the students perform the experiment with modern lab equipment or in an experimental archaeology fashion should be guided by time available, resources, and environmental control conditions (for example, recreating a smelting setting of bronze age requires an outdoor space!). In either setting, the control variables are easy to observe (temperature, condition of fluxing). There are several resources online describing this activity that are reported in the internet resource at the end of this lesson.

There are of course other experiments that can be done in a short amount of time to illustrate the process and the control on mineral separation including heap leaching, flotation, etc. The choice should be guided by the teacher's ease with the topic or the availability of a guest teacher to perform or guide the class on the experiment. Prepared sets for element separation are available from Science Supplies as separation from a mixture kits such as https://www.carolina.com/stem-kits/carolina-stem-challenge-separation-of-a-mixture-kit/820109.pr.

Mathematics Connections

Teacher will explain the concepts of imports and exports and students will discuss their views on the U.S.'s imports and export of minerals and compare their calculations from the investigation.

ELA Connections

Teachers will explain the research process and discuss how to collect and organize information for the group mineral study project. Teacher can use the Research Grid to model how to collect information and look at the ideas across sources. Students can make a similar grid in their science notebooks to support their note taking [See https://owl.english.purdue.edu/owl/resource/677/01/ for support in teaching the research process].

Social Studies Connections

Teacher will explain the concept of "economic interest" in relationship to minerals and students can create a bar graph of how much the mineral they are researching has been used over time to analyze the economic impact of that mineral.

EXTEND/APPLY KNOWLEDGE

Science Class

Students will hold a gallery walk to share their posters, similar to a professional conference. Students will peer review each other's posters, posting notes using prompts such as "I wonder . . . I notice . . . I like . . ." After the gallery walk, have a general discussion about themes across the posters and generate questions. Students should have the opportunity to answer any critical questions that their peers may have posed during the gallery walk. See http://www.theteachertoolkit.com/index.php/tool/gallery-walk for more ideas for how to use a gallery walk.

Mathematics Connections

Students can create a bar graph of the minerals used in a cell phone and use bars above the x-axis to represent minerals mined in the U.S. and bars below the x-axis to represent minerals imported from other countries.

ELA Connections

Students will use the research grid provided at the end of this lesson to take notes and continue reading about their minerals and generating and answering questions. A guest speaker, perhaps from the local USGS office, can be invited in for students to ask questions about mining. Questions can be prepared ahead of time from the research grids.

Social Studies Connections

Students can investigate global production and consumption of the mineral they are researching and include any economic and environmental challenges or benefits to areas where these minerals are located.

The process of retrieving, refining, and distributing mineral resources offers opportunities for reflective thinking, bringing the students to confront issues in environmental and social justice. For mineral resources, springing off the map of the distribution of mineral resources in the world (https://mrdata.usgs.gov/major-deposits/map-us.html#home) and/or off the mineral resources on the cell phone, teachers can ask the students to conduct research about the social and economic conditions of the countries in the world where certain mineral commodities are mined. It should become evident soon that many countries with the richest mineral commodities resources may have challenges regarding social justice and protecting the environment. Students realize that mineral resource exploitation is not transparent, it does affect the ecosystem, the poor, and those most vulnerable; students will also realize its impact will likely last beyond the operating life of the mining site. Yet, mining could and should positively contribute to sustainable development of poorer countries. Exploring the topic of social and environmental justice in mining can be daunting, but instructors could simply ask the students; if they were to be gold mine workers where in the world would they choose to go to work, and why? (Mineral education Coalition, Cell phone mini lesson).

There are many excellent topics that can be addressed under this section: conflict minerals, exploitation of children in mining, issues with recycling of e-waste, issues with disposal of mining overburden and tailings, etc.

EVALUATE/ASSESSMENT

Research Question Grid
Vocabulary Knowledge Chart
Poster Presentation

INTERNET RESOURCES

Ad Lit Website http://www.adlit.org/strategies/22093/

Directed- Reading Activity- http://www.nea.org/tools/directed-reading-think ing-activity.html).http://www.nea.org/tools/directed-reading-thinking-activity.html).

Earth Magazine found at http://www.earthmagazine.org

Evaluating Resources http://www.schrockguide.net/critical-evaluation.html

Gapminder: a fact-based worldview. www.gapminder.org.

MineralResources:https://www.mineraleducationcoalition.org/k-12-education

PBS: http://www.pbs.org/wgbh/amex/canyon/peopleevents/pandeAMEX06.html

How do we extract minerals https://www.usgs.gov/faqs/how-do-we-extract-minerals?qt-news_science_products=0#qt-news_science_products

How to teach the extraction of metals: https://edu.rsc.org/cpd/the-extraction-of-metals/4010857.article

Copper refining experiment (lab setting): https://edu.rsc.org/resources/extracting-metals-from-rocks/478.article

Ore extraction from the Ck-12 foundation: https://www.ck12.org/earth-science/ore-extraction/lesson/Extracting-Ores-MS-ES/

Copper smelting in a pit: https://www.youtube.com/watch?v=8uHc4Hirexc

Separation of copper from ore (in class) from Caterpillar: http://s7d2.scene7.com/is/content/Caterpillar/C10524704

Separation of Iron by floatation: https://www.youtube.com/watch?v=kEqYEgvlvDQ

Extraction of iron by oxidation: https://edu.rsc.org/resources/extraction-of-iron-on-a-match-head/722.article

Purdue Owl Website: https://owl.english.purdue.edu/owl/resource/677/01/

Teacher Toolkit Website: http://www.theteachertoolkit.com/index.php/tool/gallery-walk

U.S. Geological Survey website http://minerals.usgs.gov

Vocabulary: http://www.adlit.org/article/40345/

Research Question Grid (Fisher and Frey, 2012)

Students can use this grid to take notes across sources. The grid can be expanded to add more questions or more sources. Students should recreate the grid in their science notebooks to match their research questions and sources. The teacher should model how to use this grid.

	Question 1	Question 2	Question 3	Question 4
Source 1				
Source 2				
Source 3				

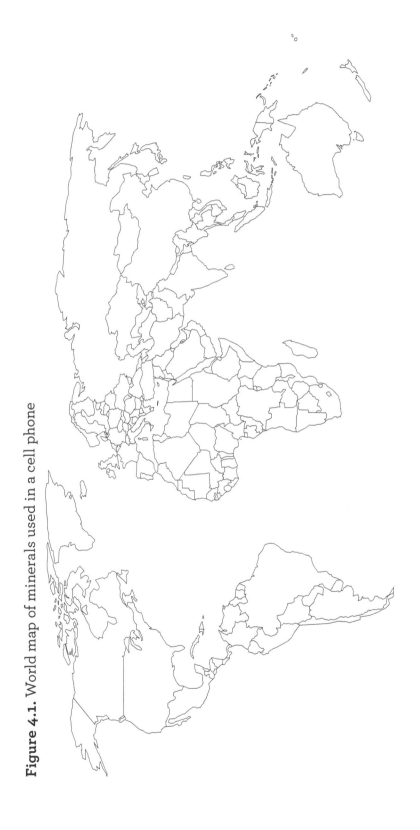

Figure 4.1. World map of minerals used in a cell phone

Vocabulary Knowledge Chart

This strategy gives students an opportunity to rate their knowledge of vocabulary needed for the lessons. Teachers can provide words for students at the beginning of the unit and students can also record words they come into contact with as they read. Students should mark their initial level of knowledge of the word and then work during the unit to move their knowledge level to the final column for each word selected.

Word	No Clue	Have heard of it	Can define it	Can give an example

Argumentation Graphic Organizer

Problem/Question:

⇩

Original Claim:

⇩

	Evidence	Reasoning
1		
2		
3		

⇩

Evidence Number	Rebuttal	Valid	Rationale

⇩

Conclusion:

Rubric for Verbal Argumentation (whole class or small group)

Characteristic	Emerging (1)	Proficient (2)	Exemplary (3)
Follows guidelines of intellectual discussion and is civil	Criticizes other people personally instead of being critical of ideas; doesn't use appropriate language	Challenges the idea but without reason; uses appropriate language	Challenges the idea with solid reasoning; uses appropriate language; diverts any unproductive discussion
Makes claim	Claim unoriginal AND indirectly related to topic	Claim original AND indirectly related to topic	Claim original AND directly related to topic
Uses reliable sources for evidence	Uses unreliable resources (such as a blog)	Only uses textbook as resource	Uses outside reliable resources (such as a scientific journal or .gov or .edu website)
Appropriate level of evidence	Opinion-based evidence	One piece of researched evidence	More than one piece of researched evidence
Responds to the content of the discussion	No response or unrelated to claim	Response is indirectly associated with claim	Response is aligned with claim
Connects with what prior person says	Unrelated to current discussion	Stay on topic, but makes no connection with person before them	Acknowledges prior person's idea and elaborates on what previous person says
Able to defend their claim/rebuttal	Has no response	Has a response but cannot back up response	Has a response and is able to back up response with further evidence
Uses appropriate reasoning	Reasoning is disconnected from claim	Reasoning is superficially connected to claim	Reasoning directly connects claim to evidence

Rubric for Poster Session

	Did not meet expectations	Approaching	Meets	Exceeds
Content Knowledge	Demonstrates little or no understanding of the content presented.	Demonstrates a partial understanding of the content presented.	Demonstrates a satisfactory understanding of the content presented.	Demonstrates an exemplary understanding of the content presented.
Accuracy	Inaccuracies in explanations.	Some problem with accuracy; may contain irrelevant details.	Most information is accurate and relevant.	All information is accurate and relevant.
Organization	Information is weakly organized; difficult to follow ideas due to manner of presentation.	Information is not clearly organized and details and connections between sections may be hard to follow.	Information is mostly organized and presented in a mostly logical manner.	Information is highly organized and presented in a logical manner.
Readability	Little to no attendance to spelling, grammar, and punctuation; excessive number of errors.	Partial attendance to spelling, grammar, and punctuation; mistakes.	Satisfactory attendance to spelling, grammar, and punctuation; some mistakes.	Exemplary attendance to spelling, grammar, and punctuation; no or very few mistakes.

Comments:

Lesson Plan 2
Mineral Resources: The Impact on Society

LESSON TWO SUMMARY

Students will develop a deeper understanding of mineral resources by analyzing design solutions for extracting minerals and processing the mineral commodity from the Earth.

ESSENTIAL QUESTION(S)

What are the types of mining?
How does mining impact the environment?
What happens when a mineral resource is depleted in a mine?
Where are mines located?
How is the best mining procedure determined for a specific mineral resource?

ESTABLISHED GOALS/OBJECTIVES

At the conclusion of this lesson, students will be able to:

- Explain mining and give examples of various types of mining.

- Compare and contrast extraction methods for obtaining minerals from the Earth.

- Analyze the costs and benefits of various mining techniques.

- Analyze and explain the environmental impact of mining.

- Discuss potential solutions for minimizing the impact on the environment.

- Calculate the cost-benefit ratios for a mining operation.

- Design a device for developing more sustainable practices for mining specific mineral resource (i.e. copper for generators or silicon for photovoltaic cells).

- Write an opinion article, using evidence to support ideas.

TIME REQUIRED

10 days (approximately 45 minutes per day; Days 7–16 in the schedule)

NECESSARY MATERIALS

Internet access

Table 4.3. Standards Addressed in STEM Road Map Module
Lesson Two

NEXT GENERATION SCIENCE STANDARDS
PERFORMANCE EXPECTATIONS

HS-PS3–3 Design, build, and refine a device that works within given constraints to convert one form of energy into another form of energy

HS- ESS3–2 Evaluate competing design solutions for developing, managing, and utilizing energy and mineral resources based on cost-benefit ratios.

DISCIPLINARY CORE IDEAS

PS3.A: Definitions of Energy

At the macroscopic scale, energy manifests itself in multiple ways, such as in motion, sound, light, and thermal energy.

PS3.D: Energy in Chemical Processes

Although energy cannot be destroyed, it can be converted to less useful forms—for example, to thermal energy in the surrounding environment.

ESS3.A: Natural Resources

All forms of energy production and other resource extraction have associated economic, social, environmental, and geopolitical costs and risks as well as benefits. New technologies and social regulations can change the balance of these factors.

ETS1.A: Defining and Delimiting an Engineering Problem

Criteria and constraints also include satisfying any requirements set by society, such as taking issues of risk mitigation into account, and they should be quantified to the extent possible and stated in such a way that one can tell if a given design meets them. (secondary)

Humanity faces major global challenges today, such as the need for supplies of clean water and food or for energy sources that minimize pollution, which can be addressed through engineering. These global challenges also may have manifestations in local communities.

ETS1.B: Developing Possible Solutions

When evaluating solutions, it is important to take into account a range of constraints, including cost, safety, reliability, and aesthetics, and to consider social, cultural, and environmental impacts. (secondary)

CROSSCUTTING CONCEPTS
Energy and Matter

Changes of energy and matter in a system can be described in terms of energy and matter flows into, out of, and within that system.

Continued

Table 4.3. (*continued*)

> *Connections to Engineering Technology, and Applications of Science*
>
> Influence of Science, Engineering and Technology on Society and the Natural World
>
> Modern civilization depends on major technological systems. Engineers continuously modify these technological systems by applying scientific knowledge and engineering design practices to increase benefits while decreasing costs and risks.
>
> Analysis of costs and benefits is a critical aspect of decisions about technology.
>
> *Connections to Nature of Science*
>
> Science Addresses Questions About the Natural and Material World
>
> Science and technology may raise ethical issues for which science, by itself, does not provide answers and solutions.
>
> Science knowledge indicates what can happen in natural systems—not what should happen. The latter involves ethics, values, and human decisions about the use of knowledge.
>
> Many decisions are not made using science alone, but rely on social and cultural contexts to resolve issues.
>
> SCIENCE AND ENGINEERING PRACTICES
>
> *Constructing Explanations and Designing Solutions*
>
> Constructing explanations and designing solutions in 9–12 builds on K–8 experiences and progresses to explanations and designs that are supported by multiple and independent student-generated sources of evidence consistent with scientific ideas, principles, and theories.
>
> Design, evaluate, and/or refine a solution to a complex real-world problem, based on scientific knowledge, student-generated sources of evidence, prioritized criteria, and tradeoff considerations.
>
> *Engaging in Argument from Evidence*
>
> Engaging in argument from evidence in 9–12 builds on K–8 experiences and progresses to using appropriate and sufficient evidence and scientific reasoning to defend and critique claims and explanations about natural and designed world(s). Arguments may also come from current scientific or historical episodes in science.
>
> Evaluate competing design solutions to a real-world problem based on scientific ideas and principles, empirical evidence, and logical arguments regarding relevant factors (e.g. economic, societal, environmental, ethical considerations).
>
> *COMMON CORE MATHEMATICS STANDARDS*
>
> MATHEMATICS PRACTICES
>
> MP1 Make sense of problems and persevere in solving them.
>
> MP2 Reason abstractly and quantitatively.

MP3 Construct viable arguments and critique the reasoning of others.

MP4 Model with mathematics.

MP5 Use appropriate tools strategically.

MP6 Attend to precision.

COMMON CORE ENGLISH/LANGUAGE ARTS STANDARDS

READING STANDARDS

R111–12.1 Cite strong and thorough textual evidence to support analysis of what the text says explicitly as well as inferences drawn from the text, including determining where the text leaves matters uncertain.

R111–12.2 Determine two or more central ideas of a text and analyze their development over the course of the text, including how they interact and build on one another to provide a complex analysis; provide an objective summary of the text.

R111–12.3 Analyze a complex set of ideas or sequence of events and explain how specific individuals, ideas, or events interact and develop over the course of the text.

R111–12.4 Determine the meaning of words and phrases as they are used in a text, including figurative, connotative, and technical meanings; analyze how an author uses and refines the meaning of a key term or terms over the course of a text (e.g., how Madison defines faction in Federalist No. 10).

R111–12.6 Determine an author's point of view or purpose in a text in which the rhetoric is particularly effective, analyzing how style and content contribute to the power, persuasiveness or beauty of the text.

R111–12.10 By the end of grade 11, read and comprehend literary nonfiction in the grades 11-CCR text complexity band proficiently, with scaffolding as needed at the high end of the range.

WRITING STANDARDS

W11–12.1a Introduce precise, knowledgeable claim(s), establish the significance of the claim(s), distinguish the claim(s) from alternate or opposing claims, and create an organization that logically sequences claim(s), counterclaims, reasons, and evidence.

W11–12.1b Develop claim(s) and counterclaims fairly and thoroughly, supplying the most relevant evidence for each while pointing out the strengths and limitations of both in a manner that anticipates the audience's knowledge level, concerns, values, and possible biases.

W11–12.1c Use words, phrases, and clauses as well as varied syntax to link the major sections of the text, create cohesion, and clarify the relationships between claim(s) and reasons, between reasons and evidence, and between claim(s) and counterclaims.

W11–12.1d Establish and maintain a formal style and objective tone while attending to the norms and conventions of the discipline in which they are writing.

Continued

Table 4.3. (*continued*)

W11–12.1e Provide a concluding statement or section that follows from and supports the argument presented.

W11–12.2a Introduce a topic; organize complex ideas, concepts, and information so that each new element builds on that which precedes it to create a unified whole; include formatting (e.g., headings), graphics (e.g., figures, tables), and multimedia when useful to aiding comprehension.

W11–12.2b Develop the topic thoroughly by selecting the most significant and relevant facts, extended definitions, concrete details, quotations, or other information and examples appropriate to the audience's knowledge of the topic.

W11–12.2c Use appropriate and varied transitions and syntax to link the major sections of the text, create cohesion, and clarify the relationships among complex ideas and concepts.

W11–12.2d Use precise language, domain-specific vocabulary, and techniques such as metaphor, simile, and analogy to manage the complexity of the topic.

W11–12.2e Establish and maintain a formal style and objective tone while attending to the norms and conventions of the discipline in which they are writing.

W11 12.2f Provide a concluding statement or section that follows from and supports the information or explanation presented (e.g., articulating implications or the significance of the topic).

W.11–12.4 Produce clear and coherent writing in which the development, organization, and style are appropriate to task, purpose, and audience.

W.11–12.5 Develop and strengthen writing as needed by planning, revising, editing, rewriting, or trying a new approach, focusing on addressing what is most significant for a specific purpose and audience.

W.11–12.8 Gather relevant information from multiple authoritative print and digital sources, using advanced searches effectively; assess the strengths and limitations of each source in terms of the task, purpose, and audience; integrate information into the text selectively to maintain the flow of ideas, avoiding plagiarism and overreliance on any one source and following a standard format for citation.

SPEAKING AND LISTENING STANDARDS

SL.11–12.1a Come to discussions prepared, having read and researched material under study; explicitly draw on that preparation by referring to evidence from texts and other research on the topic or issue to stimulate a thoughtful, well-reasoned exchange of ideas.

SL.11–12.1b Work with peers to promote civil, democratic discussions and decision-making, set clear goals and deadlines, and establish individual roles as needed.

SL.11–12.2 Integrate multiple sources of information presented in diverse formats and media (e.g., visually, quantitatively, orally) in order to make informed decisions and solve problems, evaluating the credibility and accuracy of each source and noting any discrepancies among the data.

SL.11–12.4 Present information, findings, and supporting evidence, conveying a clear and distinct perspective, such that listeners can follow the line of reasoning, alternative or opposing perspectives are addressed, and the organization, development, substance, and style are appropriate to purpose, audience, and a range of formal and informal tasks.

LITERACY STANDARDS

L.11–12.1 Demonstrate command of the conventions of standard English grammar and usage when writing or speaking.

L.11–12.2 Demonstrate command of the conventions of standard English capitalization, punctuation, and spelling when writing.

L.11–12.2a Observe hyphenation conventions.

L.11–12.2a Spell correctly.

L.11–12.3a Vary syntax for effect, consulting references

L.11–12.6 Acquire and use accurately general academic and domain-specific words and phrases, sufficient for reading, writing, speaking, and listening at the college and career readiness level; demonstrate independence in gathering vocabulary knowledge when considering a word or phrase important to comprehension or expression.

21ST CENTURY SKILLS

Creativity and Innovation, Critical Thinking and Problem Solving, Communication and Collaboration, Information Literacy, Media Literacy, ICT Literacy, Flexibility and Adaptability, Initiative and Self-Direction, Social and Cross Cultural Skills, Productivity and Accountability, Leadership and Responsibility

Table 4.4. Key Vocabulary for Lesson Two

Key Vocabulary*	Definition
Cost-benefit ratio	The calculation of a cost of an endeavor divided by a financial estimate of benefits of the endeavor.
Reclamation	Using land previously used for mining for a new purpose that benefits the community.
Recycle	Converting material previously used by a consumer into another usable material.
Sustainable	Able to maintain and continue in a way that is efficient and manageable.
Opinion Article	A piece of writing that expresses opinions about a popular topic (op ed).

* Vocabulary terms are provided for both teacher and student use. Teachers may choose to introduce all or some terms to students.

TEACHER BACKGROUND INFORMATION

The teacher should have a solid understanding of the challenges and issues associated with discovering, producing, and consuming mineral resources. The document *The US Geological Survey Energy and Minerals Science Strategy a Resource Lifecycle Approach (http://pubs.usgs.gov/circ/1383d/circ1383-D.pdf)* produced by the USGS provides current goals in the field for management and production of mineral resources. These goals include:

- Understand fundamental earth processes that form energy and mineral resources

- Understand the environmental behavior of energy and mineral resources and their waste products

- Provide inventories and assessments of energy and mineral resources

- Understand the effects of energy and mineral development on natural resources and society

- Understand the reliability and availability of energy and mineral supplies

This 34-page document further provides information about major questions about each goal and strategic actions for each goal. For example, under the goal regarding the reliability and availability of energy and mineral supplies, the document discusses how sudden disruptions such as natural hazards (earthquakes, floods) or human disruption (terrorist attacks or human errors) might impact supply chains and goes on to give actions that might mitigate energy and mineral loss.

The emphasis in this lesson should be on understanding the impact of using mineral resources and considering the cost-benefit ratio of a particular design solution for any aspect regarding extraction, refining, and distributing of mineral resources to markets worldwide.

For more background, the teacher should preview the 22-minute Ground Rules video (https://www.cat.com/en_US/by-industry/mining/SafetySustainability1/Ground Rules.html), which the students will be watching in class and lays a foundational understanding of mining. Additionally, teachers should be able to execute a Structured Academic Controversy (SAC) lesson. SAC lessons are discussions that move students beyond either/or debates into a more nuanced historical analysis. This type of lesson shifts the goal from winner classroom discussions to understanding alternative hypotheses and formulated historical synthesis. Students work in pairs to read about information to address a question for one position of the debate and form their argument. Then pairs come together in a 4-person team to discuss the two varied positions.

Typically, teachers should prepare about 4 documents per position to say in the recommended time period. The student tasks for SAC have 3 steps:

1. Partners **prepare** their side of the argument.

2. Team A joins with Team B to **present position**. Team A presents their position with evidence from documents. Team B restates Team A's position, then Team A confirms their accuracy or corrects misstatements. Team B presents their position with evidence from documents. Team A restates Team B's position, then Team B confirms their accuracy or corrects misstatements.

3. Both teams **abandon their initial positions and build consensus** using supporting evidence.

Teachers who would like to learn more about SAC can navigate to http://teaching history.org/teaching-materials/teaching-guides/21731. Teachers can emphasize the nature of science in this phase of the learning by showing how information generated in science is formed through empirical evidence and logic.

LESSON PREPARATION

The teacher should preview the videos for the lesson, and have a checklist or rubric for the key points that should be elicited by the students during class discussions. The teacher should have materials gathered for students to use for their prototypes for the mineral extraction projects. Materials can include paper, aluminum foil, boxes, tubes, string, and tape. Alternatively, teachers can ask students to bring in their own materials.

LEARNING PLAN COMPONENTS
Introductory Activity/Engagement
Science class

Connections to the Challenge: Begin each day of this lesson by directing students' attention to the driving question for the module and challenge, asking "How does mining affect the environment? How much of the mineral resources in the Earth are left for future generations?" Hold a brief student discussion of how their learning in the previous days' lesson(s) contributed to their ability to create their innovation for the final challenge. You may wish to hold a class discussion, creating a class list of key ideas on chart paper or the board, or you may wish to have students create a STEM Research Notebook entry with this information.

Students will watch the video *Ground Rules: Mining for a Sustainable Future* (*https://www.cat.com/en_US/by-industry/mining/SafetySustainability1/GroundRules.html*).

This video explains the conflicts that arise when the demand for mined minerals increases and what all people must understand about working together to meet the needs while protecting the environment. The video explains the development of new and operating mines from the perspectives of geologists, engineers, and mine managers. An example mine that was successful in terms of sustainable production is used as a template to build the protocols for further mine development around the world. Specifically, sites in Australia, Canada, Chile, Ghana, Indonesia, and the United States are discussed. Students should take notes in their STEM Research Notebook about the important ideas in the video so that they have some prepared ideas for the fishbowl discussion to follow the video.

The teacher should hold a fishbowl discussion afterward (see https://www.facinghistory.org/for-educators/educator-resources/teaching-strategies/fishbowl) to generate more research questions for the mineral team projects. The goal of a fishbowl discussion is to have all students participate in a discussion that will bring up questions or ideas that students can further explore.

In a fishbowl discussion, 6–12 students should be seated in a circle. The students in the circle are considered to be inside the fishbowl and the remainder of the students should stand around the chairs outside of the fishbowl. Students spend about 15 minutes in the fishbowl discussing the question using their notes from the video. Students standing outside of the fishbowl should take additional notes on what they want to discuss based on their observations of the fishbowl discussion. Then after 15 minutes, the students should switch and the students who have not yet been in the fishbowl take the seats and continue the discussion based on the guiding questions. Students should begin with the opening question and more questions will emerge as the discussion progresses.

1. Have students consider the following opening question: How do we balance the need for more minerals and the destruction of the Earth to get to these mineral resources?

2. Fishbowl participants discuss for 15 minutes using their video notes. Students outside of the fishbowl should take additional notes in their STEM Research Notebook based on the ideas that emerge from the discussion.

3. Students should switch positions from inside the fishbowl to outside the fishbowl. If there are still students who have not yet been inside the fishbowl, do another round before switching again.

4. Fishbowl participants discuss for 15 minutes using their video notes. Students outside of the fishbowl should take additional notes in their STEM Research Notebook based on the ideas that emerge from the discussion.

5. When all students have had at least one turn inside the fishbowl, have a whole group discussion reflecting on the main points. Write the main points of the discussion on the board so that students can summarize the work in their STEM Research Notebooks. Students will use these ideas when they produce their websites for the challenge in Lesson Three.

During this part of the lesson, the teacher should help students generate guiding questions to further their understanding about the role of mining in society and the challenges and issues associated with managing the use of mineral resources. Students should take notes on this discussion in their STEM Research Notebooks. These notes will be used later in Lesson Three for the challenge.

Mathematics Connections

Students will investigate how to calculate a cost-benefit ratio from an analysis for mining their chosen mineral. A cost-benefit analysis occurs when one makes an assessment of the benefits and the costs to a project, determining how to maximize benefits and reduce costs. The purpose of a cost-benefit analysis helps one decide whether to undertake a particular project, reframe project objectives, develop appropriate measure of success for a project, and estimates the resources needed for a particular project.

To conduct a cost benefit analysis students must be prepared to estimate benefits and costs in dollar amounts.

The main aspect to consider with respect to the availability of a resource in a certain area is the "grade" of the resources and it is calculated as amount of the resource/ amount of the rock containing it (ore) x 100. Typical ore grade of modern mines varies, for example, for copper, which we have considered in previous examples, ore grade is 0.6% (meaning, worth extracting at or above that concentration). The higher the grade, the less the amount of material that will be removed from the resource before refining, the lower the costs of extraction.

Other straightforward costs can be added when considering what equipment must be used, how much it costs to deploy and retrieve equipment to and from the mining site and to keep mining operations running. Other direct costs are the wages of personnel, cost of operations on the mining site, and insurance. Other factors may not be so straightforward when considering indirect benefits or costs such as employee satisfaction and problems that might be encountered during the mining operations with interaction with the local environment and population. Have students estimate all items in their cost-benefit analysis quantitatively in dollar amounts, whether they are direct or indirect. Students must provide a rationale for each item estimation. Students can record their cost-benefit analysis on an electronic tool, such as a spreadsheet, or can record it by hand in their STEM Research Notebook.

Students should form small groups and take the following steps in performing their cost-benefit analysis:

1. Brainstorm all known (or identified) costs and benefit items for the lifetime of the project

2. Assign quantitative dollar amounts to each of the cost and benefit items

3. Compare the costs and benefits using this formula

   a. Total benefits – total costs = outcome amount

   b. Total cost/total benefits = length of payback period (how long it will take to get a profit); Include the parties that bear the costs and the parties that reap the benefits

After groups have calculated their cost-benefit analysis, have the groups present for whole class feedback. Care should be taken that this group discussion, rather than being an information exchange, should focus on evaluation of the cost-benefit analysis. Conduct a discussion on the drawbacks of this type of analysis, mainly focusing on the inaccuracy of estimation of amounts and range of parameters that may affect the B/C ratio analysis, such as stock market sudden changes, socio-political upheaval, and natural hazards (from Lesson 1).

For teacher resources on how to conduct a cost-benefit analysis, teachers can refer to the following resources:

http://www.dummies.com/how-to/content/performing-a-costbenefit-analysis.html A brief overview of cost-benefit analysis considerations

http://management.about.com/cs/money/a/CostBenefit.htm Another overview featuring an example similar to the problem students will engage with in this lesson

Students will revise their cost-benefit analysis as they design their machines in science class on days 11–15.

ELA Connections

Students will discuss the potential impact of mining on the environment and society and brainstorm a list of pros and cons about mining practices. Students should use their notes from the prior activities in their STEM Research Notebooks and add to these notes as needed by doing additional Internet investigations. Remind students to cite their sources and write these citations into their STEM Research Notebooks so that they can be used for the Website Challenge.

When students are finished compiling their pros and cons, have them form small groups and create a poster that ranks the pros and cons from most important to least important. Students in the groups will most likely have different ideas about the ranking, so they must discuss and convince each other of the importance until they reach consensus for their poster. Once the posters are finished, have half of the class present their posters to the other half of the class in a poster session. Then switch presenters until all students have presented their posters. Conclude the activity by holding a discussion about the most common important pros and cons and least important pros and cons across the class.

Social Studies Connections

Students should work individually to map locations of deposits and mining of the mineral they are researching. Have students use a world map template that can be printed from Creative Commons websites to perform their mapping activity. Have students use a legend to explain which symbols indicate reserves and which symbols indicate current mines. To enhance this activity, students can indicate the length of time the mines have been established with different symbols or colors. In their research on their particular mineral, students may have learned more about prospective reserves or other information, which they can include on their maps. Have students analyze the maps to make written recommendations for future mining sites that will be the most productive, yet sustainable to the Earth. Students should write their recommendations for future mining in their STEM Research Notebooks. Have students who have the same minerals compare their maps and recommendations and discuss. Encourage students to revise their recommendations after they have discussed them with others.

Students can use the "Mineral Resources" tab from the USGS website (http:// mrdata.usgs.gov/) which provides several maps showing mineral deposits and mining locations.

ACTIVITY/INVESTIGATION
Science Class

By the end of Lesson Two, Students will work in teams of two to design a geo-friendly tool in order to extract a mineral resource (students must design it, but are not required to build it). Students who want to build their model tool can use the materials that the teacher provides (paper, aluminum foil, boxes, tubes, string, and tape) or have students bring in their own materials for the model. Students should work in the same pairs that worked together in lesson one, and design their tool around their knowledge of the mineral resource gathered in lesson one. Students should spend days 8–10 further researching their mineral and the current extraction methods for that mineral.

Students will need background knowledge about mineral resource extraction (more fully explained in the "explain" section of this lesson), so this information should be presented to students on day 8. Students should investigate the mining process for their selected mineral resource. On day 11, student teams will begin planning an extraction procedure or a device that is geo-friendly.

Students should design their devices with the rubric found at the end of this lesson in mind. Students need to consider why their device/procedure is better for the environment than other devices, specifically addressing some of the environmental, safety, and effectiveness concerns of current mineral extraction methods. Students should design a device that would be possible to build if they had access to the time and money resources and should rely on existing technology (i.e. the device does not rely on technology that does not exist, like teleportation). They must be able to explain why their device is a better option, but should also acknowledge any apparent disadvantages of their new device. The materials students would use to build their device should be considered. Most importantly, the new device should be able to accomplish the task it is designed to accomplish.

Students should then develop presentations of approximately three to five minutes which explain their design and the rationale behind the design. This will serve as an opportunity for students to receive peer feedback on their designs. Students should give these presentations to the entire class. While others are presenting, students should take notes on the design being presented and then provide feedback on the design or ask questions about the design. Student groups should then use the feedback they received to reconsider important elements of their designs, and revise their plans accordingly. Final student plans should be turned in for grading on the final day of the lesson, day 16, and students will present on their finalized solutions at the end of Lesson Three.

Mathematics Connections

Students should revise their calculations for the cost-benefit analysis of their design solutions for extracting their mineral. Since students first did a cost-benefit analysis for the general idea of mining their chosen mineral, they can use the skills they learned from that general activity to produce a cost-benefit analysis for this specific tool. Students will research the cost of mining the mineral(s) needed for their design, estimate the per-unit cost of their design, and compare this estimate to the price for which they believe they can sell their unit. Students should consider one-time purchases, like equipment and land rights, deployment of mining machinery, and supporting infrastructures along with recurring costs like fuel for their machines, maintenance, wages and insurances, and the costs of refining (if doable in situ) and shipping the mineral either unprocessed or already refined.

Students should form small groups and take the following steps in performing their cost-benefit analysis:

1. Brainstorm all costs and benefit items for the lifetime of the project.

2. Assign quantitative dollar amounts to each of the cost and benefit items

3. Compare the costs and benefits using this formula

    a. Total benefits – total costs = outcome amount

    b. Total cost/total benefits = length of payback period (how long it will take to get a profit)

ELA Connections

Students will draft an opinion article about solutions they feel should be implemented to limit the impact of mining on the environment and/or explain the extent to which they believe the government should get involved in mineral resource management. Students should consider the impact of mining on people and environments. Students should be sure to use elements of persuasive writing in their opinion article, and should use data/evidence to support all claims. Students can use the graphic organizer for arguments found at the end of this lesson to map out their ideas for this essay. If students are interested in occupations involving mining, they can look at this U.S. Department of Labor website https://www.onetonline.org/find/quick?s= mining

Social Studies Connections

Teachers can develop a structured academic controversy (SAC) lesson in which students respond to the fundamental question of whether and to what extent the government should play a role in keeping and managing mineral resources.
    To begin the SAC lesson, ask students to consider the following question:
    What role should government have in keeping and managing mineral resources?
    Team A: Government should control ALL mining for mineral resources
    Team B: Government should control NONE of the mining for mineral resources.

1. Partners **prepare** their side of the argument.

2. Team A joins with Team B to **present position**. Team A presents their position with evidence from documents. Team B restates Team A's position, then Team A confirms their accuracy or corrects misstatements. Team B presents their

position with evidence from documents. Team A restates Team B's position, then Team B confirms their accuracy or corrects misstatements.

3. Both teams **abandon their initial positions and build consensus** using supporting evidence.

Resources for creating a structured academic controversy are found below:

http://teachinghistory.org/teaching-materials/teaching-guides/21731 A broad overview of a structured academic controversy and how to implement them in the classroom

http://serc.carleton.edu/sp/library/sac/index.html Another overview of SAC with additional examples available

EXPLAIN
Science Class

Teachers will explain the stages of the mining process and how the process is managed to control the impact on the environment. While all mining processes aim to extract a mineral resource, the mining process differs significantly depending on the mineral resource of interest, so the teacher should consider presenting an overview of the steps involved into the mining process. For a broad overview of mining processes, teachers might use this website: http://web.mit.edu/12.000/www/m2016/finalwebsite/solutions/mining.html. This will provide the students with an awareness of the complexity of the task and give them give the correct order of steps to be considered.

Specific to mining, students add additional terms to the glossary of table 4.2, adding vocabulary as ore, tailing, AMD, etc.

Management and control of the impact on the environment concerns the production of acid mine drainage (AMD) and its control. Most active mining operation have protocols for AMD control, however abandoned mines can pose problems since sulfides compounds associated with metallic mineral resources and coal can be exposed to air and generate AMD. It is easy to set up an experiment using white vinegar to simulate the acid mine drainage and then use a neutralizing agent such as antiacid tablets or pulverized limestone. Teachers can lead students in creating a diverse number of scenarios by modifying this basic setup. Start with a simple reaction in a beaker for increasing level of acidity, and move on to constructing the most likely buffer soils that will prevent the solubility by buffer effect of the soil type. Students can create a soil profile with sands of varying composition, granulometry and compaction in plastic tubs. They can generate a topography simulating an uneven terrain and a point source release of the acidified water. They can add a pH Sensitive tracer, such as pH strip paper buried an increasingly greater distance from the point source of pollution, and make models and prediction on what type of soils offer the better buffers.

An excellent review paper by RoyChowdhury et al. (2015) deals with acid mine drainage (AMD) in a descriptive way that can be shared with high school students and be used to launch a classroom discussion on the topic of mining impact. At this stage, it would be important for the instructor to share one or more case studies (depending on classroom time and dynamics) where issues related to mining impact were considered. The Environmental Protection Agency https://www.epa.gov/ offers a wealth of case studies to choose from that can be easily retrieved by entering key words on the search string; many are suitable for high school students. It is recommended that a case study be chosen in the state or county of the school where this unit is presented (see also, EPA technical paper Acid Mine drainage Prediction for a summary of cases with data from several mines in the US)

Mathematics Connections
Teacher will continue to explain cost-benefit ratio, continuing the discussion from day 7. Students should begin moving towards their own cost-benefit ratio calculations.

ELA Connections
Teachers will explain what an opinion article is and how to write one effectively, using the following steps:

- Express your opinion as the thesis and base it on researched evidence
- Have a tight focus on one issue per opinion piece
- Use the voice of reason but be personal in communicating your ideas
- Have one clear position on the idea; you can use counter arguments to rebut but explain your position in a clear way
- State your position, back it up with evidence, and conclude by restating your opinion
- Emphasize action verbs
- Write directly
- Avoid jargon

Then students will reflect on the opinion article they wrote in the prior lesson on solutions they feel should be implemented to limit the impact of mining on the environment and/or explain the extent to which they believe the government should get involved in mineral resource management. Students should revise their opinion articles based on the teacher's notes on creating an effective opinion article.

Using the new insights that they obtained by revising their first opinion article, students will read sample opinion editorial pieces (op eds) from national and local newspapers and analyze their strengths and weaknesses. Students should specifically attend to the ways in which people support their statements with personal experience or with research.

Social Studies Connections

Students should investigate historical developments of mining processes. There are several reliable Internet sources that present a brief history of mining for the past 25–30 years. These include:

- https://www.miningpeople.com.au/news/A-look-back-How-mining-has-changed-over-30-years

- https://www.azomining.com/Article.aspx?ArticleID=1339

- https://www.generalkinematics.com/blog/a-brief-history-of-mining-and-the-advancement-of-mining-technology/

- https://www.rackersequipment.com/blog/how-mining-has-evolved-over-the-years/

From these websites, some of the technology that has changed includes:

- From ancient time until about the 1980s, mining was mainly done by manual excavation, hand-held equipment, and pressurized air and water

- During the 1600s miners started to use explosives to break up rocks in quarrying operations

- Now, soil samples are taken and many hours of work have been saved by using Mobile Metal Ion detectors to identify high concentration of chemical elements in soil from a possible mineral deposit

- Electric hydraulic drilling rigs have replaced pneumatic rigs, making the mines more productive because the machinery is more accurate and bigger

- Newly developed machines can grind and crush extracted minerals with less energy than before

- Miners still use heavy machinery, but the techniques to dig are more accurate and use less energy

- geo-metallurgy is a strategy that enables mining operation enterprises to better manage and predict the life of a mining operation

- Mining safety has been a top priority and has evolved over the years

Students might consider how mining has changed over time and what other innovations have permitted these changes (such as the use of computers and modern transportation technologies). Students can use the ideas that they have learned from this activity for the development of their mining tool at the end of this lesson.

EXTEND/APPLY KNOWLEDGE
Science Class

Students will hold a class discussion on sustainable mining practices based on what they learned through their projects. Students should be permitted to discuss the discussion topics of greatest interest to them. Students should consider the larger impacts on the earth if we sustainably mine, and should also consider the potential impacts of changing mining practices. For example, if lots of people begin using the same resources in the design of new "sustainable" mining resources, what new problems might society face? What might be the cost of retraining miners who need to learn new skills? Students might also consider the costs (in terms of money and time) associated with sustainable mining and the impacts of these costs on the global economy and local communities. The teacher or a student should record important discussion points on the board, and students should also record important discussion points in their STEM Research Notebooks.

Mathematics Connections

Students can research the uses of very expensive minerals (e.g., gold, palladium, platinum, etc.) in high-tech devices and discuss how companies spend millions, if not hundreds of millions, of dollars on prototypes and still make a profit. The following open-ended problem is a hypothetical situation where students create a rational function to model such a situation.

An energy company spent $600,000,000 on the production cost of a new, state of the art, hydrogen fuel cell used in homes. The manufacturing cost for making one of these units is $16,500 (cost for the materials, production, marketing, etc.).

As the CEO of the company, you are in charge of determining how much each unit should be sold for in order to make a profit. Develop a plan for board members of your company that includes:

1. How much each unit will cost based on the number sold.

2. How much you should charge and why.

3. A table of values showing the average cost of a unit based on the number sold with the work for each calculation shown (e.g., if only one unit is sold, then that unit cost the company $600,016,500; two units would cost $600,033,000/2; etc.).

4. A graph of the data generated from the table in step 3.

5. A chart showing potential profits based on the number of units you sell.

6. Be prepared to answer any questions the board may ask you by writing down the steps you took to generate the information for the above questions.

ELA Connections

Students can search for outlets to publish their opinion articles. Students might select a local venue or might try to publish to a larger audience, either in print or online. Students should consider how their op-eds should be tailored to the audience of their chosen venue.

Social Studies Connections

Students can research the history of mining for a specific mineral resource and the consider the regulatory legislation for it. For example, students can develop a chart illustrating the various regulatory agencies involved in resource and mineral management in the U.S. Students should consider regulatory offices at the local, state, and federal levels that might impact resource management starting with the acquisition of mining rights, environmental authorization, storage of tailings, closure and post closure, and environmental monitoring. Students should consider environmental, humanitarian, and economic issues that might cause many offices to be involved in this process. Depending on the origin of the mineral resources investigated, mining law of foreign countries could be researched.

Connecting further to the theme of social justice, students could discuss the implication of a recently launched UN program on improving artisanal mining operations across the globe (UN, 2019) as they consider the hidden costs of mineral resources like gold.

EVALUATE/ASSESSMENT

Cost-Benefit Analysis Chart
Energy Device Rubric

INTERNET RESOURCES

Facing History: https://www.facinghistory.org/for-educators/educator-resources/teaching-strategies/fishbowl

National Mining Association: https://nma.org/ EPA Acid Mine Drainage Prediction https://www.epa.gov/sites/production/files/2015-09/documents/amd.pdf

US Geological Survey Mineral Resources: http://mrdata.usgs.gov/

Mining law USA https://iclg.com/practice-areas/mining-laws-and-regulations/usa

Mining las AFRICA https://www.a-mla.org/

Mining laws in Asia Comparative study: https://www.tandfonline.com/doi/abs/10.1080/02646811.1999.11433153

For information about a company that is using hydrogen fuel cells in homes see

https://www.youtube.com/watch?v=shkFDPI6kGE

UN programme on mining sector

https://www.undp.org/content/undp/en/home/news-centre/news/2019/-180-million-investment-on-gold-mining-to-tackle-health-and-envi.html

Cost-Benefit Analysis Chart

Students can create a chart like this in their science notebooks to take notes on the cost of items for their design solutions.

Item Needed	Anticipated Cost	Benefit	Decision

Energy Device Rubric

	Did not meet expectations	Approaches	Meets	Exceeds
Content Knowledge	Demonstrates little or no understanding of the content presented.	Demonstrates a partial understanding of the content presented.	Demonstrates a satisfactory understanding of the content presented.	Demonstrates an exemplary understanding of the content presented.
Accuracy	Inaccuracies in explanations.	Some problem with accuracy; may contain irrelevant details.	Most information is accurate and relevant.	All information is accurate and relevant.
Organization	Information is weakly organized; difficult to follow ideas due to manner of presentation.	Information is not clearly organized and details and connections may be hard to follow.	Information is mostly organized and presented in a mostly logical manner.	Information is organized and presented in a logical manner.
Design	Design of the device is incomplete or inaccurate; design features are not clear or may not be possible; device reflects a limited understanding of relative scientific principles.	Design of the device is acceptable; some of the design features are relevant and possible; device reflects developing understanding of relative scientific principles.	Design of the device is mostly innovative and creative; most of the design features are relevant and possible; device reflects a proficient understanding of relative scientific principles.	Design of the device is innovative and creative; all design features are relevant and possible; device reflects strong understanding of relative scientific principles.

OTHER MEASURES

Students should be able to identify reliable resources and have written evidence of their research.

Argumentation Graphic Organizer

Problem/Question:

⬇

Original Claim:

⬇

	Evidence	Reasoning
1		
2		
3		

⬇

Evidence Number	Rebuttal	Valid	Rationale

⬇

Conclusion:

Lesson Plan 3
Why should citizens understand mineral use?

LESSON THREE SUMMARY

In this lesson, students will synthesize their research and data in order to explain their understanding of mineral resources and how these are essential to products used in global society. Students should emphasize the human experience by addressing how to make informed decisions about particular design solutions for developing, managing, and using mineral resources in society. Students will analyze their prior notes from their STEM Research Notebooks and new research during this lesson to identify the key concepts and critical understandings about mineral resources they have developed in this unit.

ESSENTIAL QUESTION(S)

How do I share my knowledge about mineral resources?

What do I think people need to know?

What strategies are the most effective in encouraging people to make an informed decision about mineral resources?

ESTABLISHED GOALS/OBJECTIVES

At the conclusion of the lesson, students will be able to:

- Develop a website that informs readers about mineral resources.

- Synthesize information from multiple sources.

TIME REQUIRED

9 days (approximately 45 minutes per day; Days 17–25 in the schedule)

NECESSARY MATERIALS

Internet access
    Website development sites such as WIX or Weebly

Table 4.5. Standards Addressed in STEM Road Map Module Lesson Three

NEXT GENERATION SCIENCE STANDARDS
PERFORMANCE EXPECTATIONS
HS-PS3–3 Design, build, and refine a device that works within given constraints to convert one form of energy into another form of energy

Continued

Table 4.5. (*continued*)

HS- ESS3–2 Evaluate competing design solutions for developing, managing, and utilizing energy and mineral resources based on cost-benefit ratios.

HS-ETS1–1 Analyze a major global challenge to specify qualitative and quantitative criteria and constraints for solutions that account for societal needs and wants.

DISCIPLINARY CORE IDEAS
PS3.A: Definitions of Energy

At the macroscopic scale, energy manifests itself in multiple ways, such as in motion, sound, light, and thermal energy.

PS3.D: Energy in Chemical Processes

Although energy cannot be destroyed, it can be converted to less useful forms—for example, to thermal energy in the surrounding environment.

ESS3.A: Natural Resources

All forms of energy production and other resource extraction have associated economic, social, environmental, and geopolitical costs and risks as well as benefits. New technologies and social regulations can change the balance of these factors.

ETS1.A: Defining and Delimiting an Engineering Problem

Criteria and constraints also include satisfying any requirements set by society, such as taking issues of risk mitigation into account, and they should be quantified to the extent possible and stated in such a way that one can tell if a given design meets them. (secondary)

Humanity faces major global challenges today, such as the need for supplies of clean water and food or for energy sources that minimize pollution, which can be addressed through engineering. These global challenges also may have manifestations in local communities.

ETS1.B: Developing Possible Solutions

When evaluating solutions, it is important to take into account a range of constraints, including cost, safety, reliability, and aesthetics, and to consider social, cultural, and environmental impacts. (secondary)

CROSSCUTTING CONCEPTS
Energy and Matter

Changes of energy and matter in a system can be described in terms of energy and matter flows into, out of, and within that system.

Connections to Engineering Technology, and Applications of Science

Influence of Science, Engineering and Technology on Society and the Natural World

Modern civilization depends on major technological systems. Engineers continuously modify these technological systems by applying scientific knowledge and engineering design practices to increase benefits while decreasing costs and risks.

Engineers continuously modify these technological systems by applying scientific knowledge and engineering design practices to increase benefits while decreasing costs and risks.

Analysis of costs and benefits is a critical aspect of decisions about technology.

Connections to Nature of Science

Science Addresses Questions About the Natural and Material World

Science and technology may raise ethical issues for which science, by itself, does not provide answers and solutions.

Science knowledge indicates what can happen in natural systems—not what should happen. The latter involves ethics, values, and human decisions about the use of knowledge.

Many decisions are not made using science alone, but rely on social and cultural contexts to resolve issues.

SCIENCE AND ENGINEERING PRACTICES
Constructing Explanations and Designing Solutions

Constructing explanations and designing solutions in 9–12 builds on K–8 experiences and progresses to explanations and designs that are supported by multiple and independent student-generated sources of evidence consistent with scientific ideas, principles, and theories.

Design, evaluate, and/or refine a solution to a complex real-world problem, based on scientific knowledge, student-generated sources of evidence, prioritized criteria, and tradeoff considerations.

Engaging in Argument from Evidence

Engaging in argument from evidence in 9–12 builds on K–8 experiences and progresses to using appropriate and sufficient evidence and scientific reasoning to defend and critique claims and explanations about natural and designed world(s). Arguments may also come from current scientific or historical episodes in science.

Evaluate competing design solutions to a real-world problem based on scientific ideas and principles, empirical evidence, and logical arguments regarding relevant factors (e.g. economic, societal, environmental, ethical considerations).

Asking Questions and Defining Problems

Asking questions and defining problems in 9–12 builds on K–8 experiences and progresses to formulating, refining, and evaluating empirically testable questions and design problems using models and simulations.

Analyze complex real-world problems by specifying criteria and constraints for successful solutions.

Continued

Table 4.5. (*continued*)

COMMON CORE MATHEMATICS STANDARDS
MATHEMATICS PRACTICES

MP1 Make sense of problems and persevere in solving them.

MP2 Reason abstractly and quantitatively.

MP3 Construct viable arguments and critique the reasoning of others.

MP4 Model with mathematics.

MP5 Use appropriate tools strategically.

MP6 Attend to precision.

MP7 Look for and make use of structure.

MP8 Look for and express regularity in repeated reasoning.

MATHEMATICS CONTENT

REI.D.10 Represent and solve equations and inequalities graphically.

REI.D.11 Represent and solve equations and inequalities graphically.

COMMON CORE ENGLISH/LANGUAGE ARTS STANDARDS
READING STANDARDS

R111–12.1 Cite strong and thorough textual evidence to support analysis of what the text says explicitly as well as inferences drawn from the text, including determining where the text leaves matters uncertain.

R111–12.2 Determine two or more central ideas of a text and analyze their development over the course of the text, including how they interact and build on one another to provide a complex analysis; provide an objective summary of the text.

R111–12.3 Analyze a complex set of ideas or sequence of events and explain how specific individuals, ideas, or events interact and develop over the course of the text.

R111–12.4 Determine the meaning of words and phrases as they are used in a text, including figurative, connotative, and technical meanings; analyze how an author uses and refines the meaning of a key term or terms over the course of a text (e.g., how Madison defines faction in Federalist No. 10).

R111–12.6 Determine an author's point of view or purpose in a text in which the rhetoric is particularly effective, analyzing how style and content contribute to the power, persuasiveness or beauty of the text.

R111–12.8 Delineate and evaluate the reasoning in seminal U.S. texts, including the application of constitutional principles and use of legal reasoning (e.g., in U.S. Supreme Court majority opinions and dissents) and the premises, purposes, and arguments in works of public advocacy (e.g., The Federalist, presidential addresses).

R111–12.10 By the end of grade 11, read and comprehend literary nonfiction in the grades 11-CCR text complexity band proficiently, with scaffolding as needed at the high end of the range.

WRITING STANDARDS

W11–12.1a Introduce precise, knowledgeable claim(s), establish the significance of the claim(s), distinguish the claim(s) from alternate or opposing claims, and create an organization that logically sequences claim(s), counterclaims, reasons, and evidence.

W11–12.1b Develop claim(s) and counterclaims fairly and thoroughly, supplying the most relevant evidence for each while pointing out the strengths and limitations of both in a manner that anticipates the audience's knowledge level, concerns, values, and possible biases.

W11–12.1c Use words, phrases, and clauses as well as varied syntax to link the major sections of the text, create cohesion, and clarify the relationships between claim(s) and reasons, between reasons and evidence, and between claim(s) and counterclaims.

W11–12.1d Establish and maintain a formal style and objective tone while attending to the norms and conventions of the discipline in which they are writing.

W11–12.1e Provide a concluding statement or section that follows from and supports the argument presented.

W11–12.2a Introduce a topic; organize complex ideas, concepts, and information so that each new element builds on that which precedes it to create a unified whole; include formatting (e.g., headings), graphics (e.g., figures, tables), and multimedia when useful to aiding comprehension.

W11–12.2b Develop the topic thoroughly by selecting the most significant and relevant facts, extended definitions, concrete details, quotations, or other information and examples appropriate to the audience's knowledge of the topic.

W11–12.2c Use appropriate and varied transitions and syntax to link the major sections of the text, create cohesion, and clarify the relationships among complex ideas and concepts.

W11–12.2d Use precise language, domain-specific vocabulary, and techniques such as metaphor, simile, and analogy to manage the complexity of the topic.

W11–12.2e Establish and maintain a formal style and objective tone while attending to the norms and conventions of the discipline in which they are writing.

W11–12.2f Provide a concluding statement or section that follows from and supports the information or explanation presented (e.g., articulating implications or the significance of the topic).

W.11–12.4 Produce clear and coherent writing in which the development, organization, and style are appropriate to task, purpose, and audience.

W.11–12.5 Develop and strengthen writing as needed by planning, revising, editing, rewriting, or trying a new approach, focusing on addressing what is most significant for a specific purpose and audience.

Continued

Table 4.5. (*continued*)

W.11–12.8 Gather relevant information from multiple authoritative print and digital sources, using advanced searches effectively; assess the strengths and limitations of each source in terms of the task, purpose, and audience; integrate information into the text selectively to maintain the flow of ideas, avoiding plagiarism and overreliance on any one source and following a standard format for citation.

W.11–12.9 Draw evidence from literary or informational texts to support analysis, reflection, and research.

W.11–12.9a Apply grades 11–12 Reading standards to literature (e.g., "Demonstrate knowledge of eighteenth-, nineteenth- and early-twentieth-century foundational works of American literature, including how two or more texts from the same period treat similar themes or topics").

W.11–12.9b Apply grades 11–12 Reading standards to literary nonfiction (e.g., "Delineate and evaluate the reasoning in seminal U.S. texts, including the application of constitutional principles and use of legal reasoning (e.g., in U.S. Supreme Court Case majority opinions and dissents) and the premises, purposes, and arguments in works of public advocacy (e.g., The Federalist, presidential addresses)").

W.11–12.10 Write routinely over extended time frames (time for research, reflection, and revision) and shorter time frames (a single sitting or a day or two) for a range of tasks, purposes, and audiences.

SPEAKING AND LISTENING STANDARDS

SL.11–12.1a Come to discussions prepared, having read and researched material under study; explicitly draw on that preparation by referring to evidence from texts and other research on the topic or issue to stimulate a thoughtful, well-reasoned exchange of ideas.

SL.11–12.1b Work with peers to promote civil, democratic discussions and decision-making, set clear goals and deadlines, and establish individual roles as needed.

SL.11–12.2 Integrate multiple sources of information presented in diverse formats and media (e.g., visually, quantitatively, orally) in order to make informed decisions and solve problems, evaluating the credibility and accuracy of each source and noting any discrepancies among the data.

SL.11–12.4 Present information, findings, and supporting evidence, conveying a clear and distinct perspective, such that listeners can follow the line of reasoning, alternative or opposing perspectives are addressed, and the organization, development, substance, and style are appropriate to purpose, audience, and a range of formal and informal tasks.

LITERACY STANDARDS

L.11–12.1 Demonstrate command of the conventions of standard English grammar and usage when writing or speaking.

L.11–12.1a Apply the understanding that usage is a matter of convention, can change over time, and is sometimes contested.

L.11–12.1b Resolve issues of complex or contested usage, consulting references (e.g., Merriam-Webster's Dictionary of English Usage, Garner's Modern American Usage) as needed.

L.11–12.2 Demonstrate command of the conventions of standard English capitalization, punctuation, and spelling when writing.

L.11–12.2a Observe hyphenation conventions.

L.11–12.2a Spell correctly.

L.11–12.3a Vary syntax for effect, consulting references

L.11–12.6 Acquire and use accurately general academic and domain-specific words and phrases, sufficient for reading, writing, speaking, and listening at the college and career readiness level; demonstrate independence in gathering vocabulary knowledge when considering a word or phrase important to comprehension or expression.

21ST CENTURY SKILLS

Creativity and Innovation, Critical Thinking and Problem Solving, Communication and Collaboration, Information Literacy, Media Literacy, ICT Literacy, Flexibility and Adaptability, Initiative and Self-Direction, Social and Cross Cultural Skills, Productivity and Accountability, Leadership and Responsibility

Table 4.6. Key Vocabulary in Lesson Three

Key Vocabulary*	Definition
Coding	Using a specific language to develop a website, app, or other computer program.

* Vocabulary terms are provided for both teacher and student use. Teachers may choose to introduce all or some terms to students.

TEACHER BACKGROUND INFORMATION

Teachers should have some knowledge of how to create a website or work with another teacher or resource specialist who can help with this lesson. Some suggestions include:

- Gather the information that will be communicated on the website

- Organize the information to create one or two main messages to be communicated with evidence to back each message

- Organize information that will be on the front page and what will be on supporting pages

- Select a template that will suit the type of information that will be communicated

- Type in the information and support with images, always citing the image and using creative commons material.

Consult with an instructional technology specialist and/or see the following Internet resources for support in understanding how to design a website:

Weebly Websites: http://www.weebly.com
Wix Websites: https://www.wix.com/
WordPress Websites: https://en.support.wordpress.com/using-wordpress-to-create-a-website/
Website design instructions:https://www.how-to-build-websites.com/teach-web-design-in-middle-school.php

Teachers can emphasize the nature of science in this third lesson in the module by emphasizing how new knowledge continues to inform our understanding of how to use mineral resources in society. Encourage students to pay careful attention to what still needs to be known and think about ways to continue exploring and understanding the potential of minerals in impacting our society.

LESSON PREPARATION

Teachers should be familiar with the technology available in the school and schedule time in the computer lab or with laptops in the classroom. This is a good opportunity to partner with the technology instructor or invite parents or community members with expertise in website development to volunteer to help.

LEARNING PLAN COMPONENTS
Introductory Activity/Engagement
Science Class

Connections to the Challenge: Begin each day of this lesson by directing students' attention to the driving question for the module and challenge.

STEM Research Notebook Prompt

Ask students to respond to the following thought-provoking questions,
  Who owns the valuable mineral resource of Earth? People who own the property or the people who have the technology to extract them? How might disputes between these groups be settled?

Students should reflect on their responses to these questions and the important information should be recorded in their STEM Research Notebooks. In groups, students should discuss how their learning in the previous days' lessons contributed to their ability to create their innovation for the final challenge (as outlined in the Lesson Preparation section). You may wish to hold a class discussion, creating a class list of key ideas on chart paper or the board, or you may wish to have students create a STEM Research Notebook entry with this information. Students will review their STEM Research Notebooks and artifacts created and hold a discussion about the most important ideas they learned about mineral resources. Students can complete the reasoning chain discussion frame "I used to think . . . but now I think . . . because . . ." Students should first record these ideas in their STEM Research Notebooks and then share them with the class.

Students will review STEM Research Notebooks and artifacts created and hold a discussion about the most important ideas they learned about the potential, production, consumption, and impact of their mineral. The teacher should help guide students' thinking to develop deeper questions about mineral resources. Encourage students to revisit their science notebooks and see if all questions previously discussed have been answered. Have them observe the changes in their understanding from beginning to end and start to think about how they will convey this understanding to a broader audience by developing a website to share their learning. By the end of this lesson, students will create the completed website (additional details about this assignment to follow).

Mathematics Connections

Discuss what kind of data and visualization that students can create for their website and create timeline for completing project.

Ideas for discussion about type of data visualization:

1. Consider the audience that you want for the website and write for this audience.
2. Use general information for the first pages on the website and be more specific and detailed with data when the reader clicks deeper into the website.

ELA Connections

Students will explore careers associated with mining (geologist, surveyor, engineer, miner, etc.).

Social Studies Connections

Review resources to include in the opinion article and website and discuss proper formatting techniques.

ACTIVITY/INVESTIGATION
Science Class, Mathematics, ELA and Social Studies Connections

Students will take on the role of concerned citizens and create a website with the goal of informing citizens about mineral use and its impact on society. Students should work in groups of 3 or 4 in order to develop their websites, and should be encouraged to work in groups with people who they did not previously partner with. This will encourage sharing of information learned across different groups of people.

Students will design and develop their website according to the rubric at the end of this lesson. The topic of the website should be focused on a specific issue related to mineral use and its impact on society (rather than a broad overview of many issues that arise from mineral use). Teams should construct websites on different topics, however. To help students get started on their research design, students should consider lingering questions that were generated in previous lessons. These questions might be identified by having students reflect on their STEM Research Notebooks or on the projects they developed.

Once students settle on a topic, students should begin searching for resources related to their topic. Students should understand the issues surrounding the use of the specific mineral and discuss who is impacted by these issues. Students should also consider larger environmental concerns.

Students should use the Engineering Design Process (EDP) to create the website. Introduce the EDP to students as a process by which engineers and other STEM professionals solve problems and accomplish complex tasks (see Explain section for more information). Emphasize to students that engineers routinely work collaboratively and that they will work as teams to solve their final challenge. The EDP will provide a framework for this group work. Show students the EDP graphic (attached at the end of this lesson) and review each of the steps with students. As they plan and create their websites, they should note their progress in their STEM Research Notebooks by creating an entry for each stage of the EDP for the development of the description of the simulation.

Students should provide evidence of their use of the EDP in their STEM Research Notebooks, labeling a page with each step of the EDP and providing information appropriate to that step. You may wish to provide students with a general outline for organizing this information in their notebooks. For example:

1. Define

    a. Identify your group's target audience.

    b. What is the goal of your website (for example, the goal might be to provide information to your audience, to persuade them of something, to clarify understandings of mineral resources, to protect the public, etc.)?

    c. What products do you need to produce?

2. Learn

   a. What additional information do you need?

   b. What did you find out from your research? Remember to provide citations for your information.

   c. What ideas do team members have?

3. Plan

   a. How will you schedule your work to ensure that you complete it on time?

   b. How will you divide tasks? Hint: you might want to create a chart assigning team members jobs.

   c. What will your prototype or model be? Make a sketch of your website.

   d. What materials do you need?

4. Try

   a. Create the components of your response

      i. Goal of website

      ii. Written description of website

      iii. Storyboard of website

5. Test

   a. Practice your presentation on your website and get feedback from others if possible – make sure that your audience understands your goal!

   b. What worked well?

   c. What didn't work well?

6. Decide

   a. Based upon your test run(s) of presenting your website, what will you change?

7. Share

   a. Share your website ideas in a whole class – make sure you know who will present various parts of your presentation.

The language of the website should be similar to the opinion piece previously constructed – it should advocate for a certain position on mineral usage. Students

should consider how to present data and evidence in order to support their positions, and ensure all graphics are appropriate. Students can hyperlink to other resources as appropriate, however the website should stand alone without forcing the user to reference another website. Websites should also be pleasing to the eye and easy to navigate.

EXPLAIN
Science Class

Explain how to create a website. Teachers who are comfortable with coding are encouraged to teach their students how to code or bring in an expert that can help students with coding. If teachers are uncomfortable with this, teachers can use other programs to design the website, including online web design tools and computer programs designed for web design. Students might have extensive knowledge of website design which the teacher can use to assist with their instruction.

Mathematics Connections

Explain how mineral resources are essential to society by describing the potential, production, and consumption of the mineral and the cost-benefit analysis of various design solutions. Students should revisit their cost-benefit analysis and identify what group of people are impacted for each line item. Students should also explain the reason this group of people is impacted (both good and bad) by each line item in their cost benefit analysis. Once students have identified each group of people who are impacted by the costs and benefits of their chosen mineral extraction, they should make an estimate of the group of people who most benefit from the mineral extraction and which group of people have the most cost for the mineral extraction. Students should present an argument for their analysis by stating a claim (which group is most positively impacted and which group is most negatively impacted by the mineral extraction), backing it up with evidence and their reasoning. Students can use the graphic organizer and rubric found at the end of this lesson to help them organize their ideas for their argument.

ELA and Social Studies Connections

The teacher should explain how to write clearly and effectively for a website. The teacher should identify different genres students may use and styles that make the website friendly for readers. The teacher should also discuss the audience of the website. For example, if the website is meant to be educational, what sort of resources should be available if you want children to understand the website? Adults? Students might also consider developing the website for a specific population, like a resource website for people to turn to who live near an active mine. Students should understand the purpose of citing resources and the style that students will be expected to

follow for the website (i.e. APA, MLA). Teachers should be consistent in their citation expectations across all disciplines to help students master a single citation method.

EXTEND/APPLY KNOWLEDGE
Science Class

Teacher should hold a "conference" to show the design solutions of the products that students developed in Lesson Two. Students should present their finalized design solutions by modifying the draft presentations given during Lesson Two in order to reflect any major changes. When presenting, students should explain any change they made in their design from Lesson Two to their current design and explain why this change was made. Students should be sure that their presentations include a detailed diagram of their final designs, along with a rationale for their designs. To mimic a conference the presentations should be organized as follows:

1. Students have 15 minutes to explain their design solution and the changes that they have made since Lesson Two

2. Give the students in the audience 5 minutes to ask questions about the design solution or the changes made

3. After 3 presentations, the teacher should act like a moderator and ask the audience (whole class) to comment on similarities that exist among the three designs and things that might be optimized for all of the design solutions. Do this for each group of three presentations.

Mathematics, ELA, and Social Studies Connections

Publish the website. Students should then view one another's sites and provide feedback on changes that should be made. A rubric is provided at the end of this lesson for this purpose. Consider having student critiques via the rubric count as a grade so that critiques are as detailed as possible. After students receive written feedback on their website design, they should get back into their groups of 3 or 4 so they can redesign their websites. Students should write a 2-page reflection of their website functionality and communication effectiveness based on the feedback and redesign. The reflection should answer the following questions:

- What was your major message for the website? Was that effectively communicated? Why or why not?

- What worked well in the original design? Why did that item work well to communicate the information?

- What needed to be changed based on the student feedback? Why were these things not as effective?

- How did you address the feedback for your redesign?

- Why do you think your redesign will be more effective in communicating your message?

- What is the evidence that you used to make your claims?

- What alternative observations may seem inconsistent and why?

EVALUATE/ASSESSMENT

Website production
   Website Rubric
   Opinion Article Rubric

INTERNET RESOURCES

Dreamweaver for designing websites (http://www.adobe.com/products/dreamweaver.html)

Weebly Websites: http://www.weebly.com

WordPress Websites: https://en.support.wordpress.com/using-wordpress-to-create-a-website/

https://www.how-to-build-websites.com/teach-web-design-in-middle-school.php

Figure 4.2. Engineering Design Process

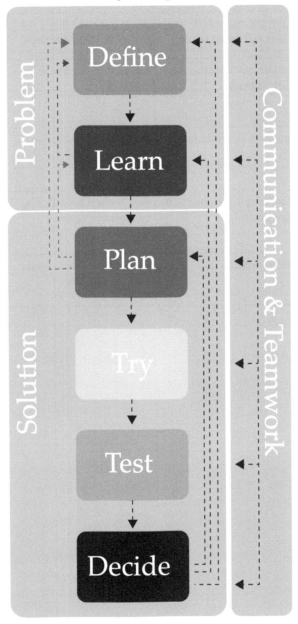

Argumentation Graphic Organizer
Rubric for Written Argument

Characteristic	Emerging (1)	Proficient (2)	Exemplary (3)
Makes claim	Claim unoriginal AND indirectly related to topic	Claim original AND indirectly related to topic	Claim original AND directly related to topic
Uses reliable sources for evidence	Uses unreliable resources (such as blog)	Only uses textbook as resource	Uses outside reliable resources (such as a scientific journal or .gov or .edu website)
Appropriate level of evidence	Opinion-based evidence	One piece of researched evidence	More than one piece of researched evidence
Uses appropriate reasoning	Reasoning is disconnected from claim	Reasoning is superficially connected to claim	Reasoning directly connects claim to evidence
Uses rebuttal	Has no rebuttal	Has a rebuttal but cannot back up response	Has a rebuttal and is able to back up response with further evidence

Website Rubric

	Did not meet expectations	Approaches	Meets	Exceeds
Communication of Ideas	Ideas are minimally developed; transitions are weak	Ideas are partially Developed; transitions are somewhat clear	Ideas are adequately developed; transitions are mostly clear	Ideas are fully developed; transitions are clear; logical order of ideas
Accuracy of Information	Multiple errors or inaccurate claims stated.	Information is partially accurate; several places with unsubstantiated claims.	Information is mostly accurate; might be a few areas needing greater evidence	Information is fully accurate; all misconceptions are addressed
Resource Use	Minimally researched; evidence weakly supports claims or conflicts with claims; resources	Partially researched; evidence somewhat supports claims; resources may be questionable	Adequately researched; evidence mostly supports claims; (at least 3) reliable resources	Well-researched; evidence fully supports claims; multiple (at least 5), reliable resources
Academic Language Use	Inappropriately or does not use at all specialized vocabulary to explain concepts	May use inappropriately or uses limited range of specialized vocabulary to explain	Appropriately uses adequate range of specialized vocabulary to explain concepts	Appropriately uses broad range of specialized vocabulary to explain concepts
Presentation	Not engaging; limited creativity; uses few tools or ineffective use of tools.	Somewhat engaging – may lack originality Uses some (at least 2) tools, some may be ineffective.	Engaging; mostly effective use of multiple at least 3) tools	Very engaging and original; creative and effective use of multiple tools (3 or more) (i.e. still pictures, voice overs, images, etc.)
Requirements	Few requirements included	Some requirements included	Most requirements included	All requirements included

Opinion Article Rubric

	Exceeds	Meets	Approaches	Did not meet expectations
Accuracy of Evidence	Provides accurate and credible information based on evidence.	Provides mostly accurate information on the topic based on evidence.	Provides some accurate information on the topic based on evidence	Does not provide accurate information on the topic or bases information on opinion only.
Organization	Ideas are very clearly and logically presented with a clear opening and well developed arguments; problem clearly defined; overall very cohesive	Ideas are presented, opening is mostly clear and problem is identified; arguments are developed. Mostly cohesive.	Ideas are presented, but organization may be unclear in parts or logic not clearly explained; problem may not be clearly identified; arguments may be underdeveloped. Somewhat cohesive.	Ideas are not developed and parts may not make sense; problem is vaguely identified; ideas are more reported versus arguments developed.
Clarity of Writing	The writing is very concise with strong, effective word choices and meaningful sentence structures; does not overuse jargon; meaning is accessible to the audience.	The writing is mostly concise with effective word choices and sentence structures; does not overuse jargon; meaning is mostly accessible to the audience.	The writing is somewhat concise with some, effective word choices and sentence structures; might use some jargon; meaning is somewhat accessible to the audience.	Writing is not concise and word choices and sentence structures interfere with clarity of meaning.
Call to Action	The article provides very clear and purposeful direction for readers on how they can make an informed decision about the topic.	The piece provides mostly clear and purposeful direction for readers on how they can make an informed decision about the topic.	The piece provides limited ideas for what readers can do to make an informed decision about the topic.	The piece does not provide a clear direction for what readers can do to make an informed decision about the topic.

REFERENCES

Fisher, D. and Frey, N. (2012). Improving adolescent literacy: Content area strategies at work. Boston, MA: Pearson.

https://mrdata.usgs.gov/major-deposits/map-us.html#home

https://mineralseducationcoalition.org/wp-content/uploads/Cell-phone-activity.pdf

Peters-Burton, E. E., Seshaiyer, P., Burton, S. R., Drake-Patrick, J., and Johnson, C. C. (2015). The STEM road map for grades 9–12. In C. C. Johnson, E. E. Peters-Burton, and T. J. Moore (Eds.), *STEM road map: A framework for integrated STEM education* (pp. 124–162). New York, NY: Routledge.

RoyChowdhury, A., Sarkar, D., and Datta, R. (2015). Remediation of Acid Mine Drainage-Impacted Water. Curr Pollution Rep 1, 131–141 https://doi.org/10.1007/s40726-015-0011-3

USGS, 2009 do we take minerals for granted? https://www.usgs.gov/energy-and-minerals/mineral-resources-program/science/do-we-take-minerals-granted?qt-science_center_objects=0#qt-science_center_objects

TRANSFORMING LEARNING WITH MINERAL RESOURCES AND THE *STEM ROAD MAP CURRICULUM SERIES*

Carla C. Johnson

This chapter serves as a conclusion to the Mineral Resources integrated STEM curriculum module, but it is just the beginning of the transformation of your classroom that is possible through use of the *STEM Road Map Curriculum Series.* In this book, many key resources have been provided to make learning meaningful for your students through integration of science, technology, engineering, and mathematics, as well as social studies and English language arts, into powerful problem- and project-based instruction. First, the Mineral Resources curriculum is grounded in the latest theory of learning for students in grade 11 specifically. Second, as your students work through this module, they engage in using the engineering design process (EDP) and build prototypes like engineers and STEM professionals in the real world. Third, students acquire important knowledge and skills grounded in national academic standards in mathematics, English language arts, science, and 21st century skills that will enable their learning to be deeper, retained longer, and applied throughout, illustrating the critical connections within and across disciplines. Finally, authentic formative assessments, including strategies for differentiation and addressing misconceptions, are embedded within the curriculum activities.

The Mineral Resources curriculum in the Optimizing the Human Condition STEM Road Map theme can be used in single-content classrooms (e.g., mathematics) where there is only one teacher or expanded to include multiple teachers and content areas across classrooms. Through the exploration of the Designing a Website for a Global Demand on Minerals Challenge, students engage in a real-world STEM problem on the first day of instruction and gather necessary knowledge and skills along the way in the context of solving the problem.

The other topics in the *STEM Road Map Curriculum Series* are designed in a similar manner, and NSTA Press and Routledge have published additional volumes in this series for this and other grade levels, and have plans to publish more.

For an up-to-date list of volumes in the series, please visit https://www.routledge.com/STEM-Road-Map-Curriculum-Series/book-series/SRM (for titles co-published by Routledge and NSTA Press), or https://www.nsta.org/book-series/stem-road-map-curriculum (for titles published by NSTA Press).

If you are interested in professional development opportunities focused on the STEM Road Map specifically or integrated STEM or STEM programs and schools overall, contact the lead editor of this project, Dr. Carla C. Johnson, Professor of Science Education at NC State University. Someone from the team will be in touch to design a program that will meet your individual, school, or district needs.

APPENDIX

CONTENT STANDARDS ADDRESSED IN STEM ROAD MAP MODULE

Table A.1. Next Generation Science Standards (NGSS)

Performance Expectations	Disciplinary Core Ideas and Crosscutting Concepts	Science and Engineering Practices
HS-PS3-3 Design, build, and refine a device that works within given constraints to convert one form of energy into another form of energy HS-ESS3-2 Evaluate competing design solutions for developing, managing, and utilizing energy and mineral resources based on cost-benefit ratios. HS-ETS1-1 Analyze a major global challenge to specify qualitative and quantitative criteria and constraints for solutions that account for societal needs and wants.	**Disciplinary Core Ideas** PS3.A: Definitions of Energy At the macroscopic scale, energy manifests itself in multiple ways, such as in motion, sound, light, and thermal energy. PS3.D: Energy in Chemical Processes Although energy cannot be destroyed, it can be converted to less useful forms—for example, to thermal energy in the surrounding environment. ESS3.A: Natural Resources All forms of energy production and other resource extraction have associated economic, social, environmental, and geopolitical costs and risks as well as benefits. New technologies and social regulations can change the balance of these factors. ETS1.A: Defining and Delimiting an Engineering Problem Criteria and constraints also include satisfying any requirements set by society, such as taking issues of risk mitigation into account, and they should be quantified to the extent possible and stated in such a way that one can tell if a given design meets them. (secondary) Humanity faces major global challenges today, such as the need for supplies of clean water and food or for energy sources that minimize pollution, which can be addressed through engineering. These global challenges also may have manifestations in local communities. ETS1.B: Developing Possible Solutions When evaluating solutions, it is important to take into account a range of constraints, including cost, safety, reliability, and aesthetics, and to consider social, cultural, and environmental impacts. (secondary) **Crosscutting Concepts** *Energy and Matter* Changes of energy and matter in a system can be described in terms of energy and matter flows into, out of, and within that system.	*Constructing Explanations and Designing Solutions* Constructing explanations and designing solutions in 9–12 builds on K–8 experiences and progresses to explanations and designs that are supported by multiple and independent student-generated sources of evidence consistent with scientific ideas, principles, and theories. Design, evaluate, and/or refine a solution to a complex real-world problem, based on scientific knowledge, student-generated sources of evidence, prioritized criteria, and tradeoff considerations. *Engaging in Argument from Evidence* Engaging in argument from evidence in 9–12 builds on K–8 experiences and progresses to using appropriate and sufficient evidence and scientific reasoning to defend and critique claims and explanations about natural and designed world(s). Arguments may also come from current scientific or historical episodes in science. Evaluate competing design solutions to a real-world problem based on scientific ideas and principles, empirical evidence, and logical arguments regarding relevant factors (e.g. economic, societal, environmental, ethical considerations).

Continued

Table A.1. (*continued*)

Connections to Engineering Technology, and Applications of Science	Asking Questions and Defining Problems
Influence of Science, Engineering and Technology on Society and the Natural World Modern civilization depends on major technological systems. Engineers continuously modify these technological systems by applying scientific knowledge and engineering design practices to increase benefits while decreasing costs and risks. *Connections to Engineering, Technology, and Applications of Science* *Influence of Science, Engineering, and Technology on Society and the Natural World* Engineers continuously modify these technological systems by applying scientific knowledge and engineering design practices to increase benefits while decreasing costs and risks. Analysis of costs and benefits is a critical aspect of decisions about technology. *Connections to Nature of Science* *Science Addresses Questions About the Natural and Material World* Science and technology may raise ethical issues for which science, by itself, does not provide answers and solutions. Science knowledge indicates what can happen in natural systems—not what should happen. The latter involves ethics, values, and human decisions about the use of knowledge. Many decisions are not made using science alone, but rely on social and cultural contexts to resolve issues.	Asking questions and defining problems in 9–12 builds on K–8 experiences and progresses to formulating, refining, and evaluating empirically testable questions and design problems using models and simulations. Analyze complex real-world problems by specifying criteria and constraints for successful solutions.

Table A.2. Common Core Mathematics and English/Language Arts (ELA) Standards

Common Core Mathematics	Common Core English/Language Arts (ELA)
Mathematics Practices MP1 Make sense of problems and persevere in solving them. MP2 Reason abstractly and quantitatively. MP3 Construct viable arguments and critique the reasoning of others. MP4 Model with mathematics. MP5 Use appropriate tools strategically. MP6 Attend to precision. MP7 Look for and make use of structure. MP8 Look for and express regularity in repeated reasoning. **Mathematics Content** REI.D.10 Represent and solve equations and inequalities graphically. REI.D.11 Represent and solve equations and inequalities graphically.	Reading Standards R111–12.1 Cite strong and thorough textual evidence to support analysis of what the text says explicitly as well as inferences drawn from the text, including determining where the text leaves matters uncertain. R111–12.2 Determine two or more central ideas of a text and analyze their development over the course of the text, including how they interact and build on one another to provide a complex analysis; provide an objective summary of the text. R111–12.3 Analyze a complex set of ideas or sequence of events and explain how specific individuals, ideas, or events interact and develop over the course of the text. R111–12.4 Determine the meaning of words and phrases as they are used in a text, including figurative, connotative, and technical meanings; analyze how an author uses and refines the meaning of a key term or terms over the course of a text (e.g., how Madison defines faction in Federalist No. 10). R111–12.6 Determine an author's point of view or purpose in a text in which the rhetoric is particularly effective, analyzing how style and content contribute to the power, persuasiveness or beauty of the text. R111–12.8 Delineate and evaluate the reasoning in seminal U.S. texts, including the application of constitutional principles and use of legal reasoning (e.g., in U.S. Supreme Court majority opinions and dissents) and the premises, purposes, and arguments in works of public advocacy (e.g., The Federalist, presidential addresses). R111–12.10 By the end of grade 11, read and comprehend literary nonfiction in the grades 11-CCR text complexity band proficiently, with scaffolding as needed at the high end of the range. Writing Standards W11–12.1a Introduce precise, knowledgeable claim(s), establish the significance of the claim(s), distinguish the claim(s) from alternate or opposing claims, and create an organization that logically sequences claim(s), counterclaims, reasons, and evidence. W11–12.1b Develop claim(s) and counterclaims fairly and thoroughly, supplying the most relevant evidence for each while pointing out the strengths and limitations of both in a manner that anticipates the audience's knowledge level, concerns, values, and possible biases.

Continued

Table A.2. (*continued*)

	W11–12.1c Use words, phrases, and clauses as well as varied syntax to link the major sections of the text, create cohesion, and clarify the relationships between claim(s) and reasons, between reasons and evidence, and between claim(s) and counterclaims.
	W11–12.1d Establish and maintain a formal style and objective tone while attending to the norms and conventions of the discipline in which they are writing.
	W11–12.1e Provide a concluding statement or section that follows from and supports the argument presented.
	W11–12.2a Introduce a topic; organize complex ideas, concepts, and information so that each new element builds on that which precedes it to create a unified whole; include formatting (e.g., headings), graphics (e.g., figures, tables), and multimedia when useful to aiding comprehension.
	W11–12.2b Develop the topic thoroughly by selecting the most significant and relevant facts, extended definitions, concrete details, quotations, or other information and examples appropriate to the audience's knowledge of the topic.
	W11–12.2c Use appropriate and varied transitions and syntax to link the major sections of the text, create cohesion, and clarify the relationships among complex ideas and concepts.
	W11–12.2d Use precise language, domain-specific vocabulary, and techniques such as metaphor, simile, and analogy to manage the complexity of the topic.
	W11–12.2e Establish and maintain a formal style and objective tone while attending to the norms and conventions of the discipline in which they are writing.
	W11–12.2f Provide a concluding statement or section that follows from and supports the information or explanation presented (e.g., articulating implications or the significance of the topic).
	W.11–12.4 Produce clear and coherent writing in which the development, organization, and style are appropriate to task, purpose, and audience.
	W.11–12.5 Develop and strengthen writing as needed by planning, revising, editing, rewriting, or trying a new approach, focusing on addressing what is most significant for a specific purpose and audience.
	W.11–12.8 Gather relevant information from multiple authoritative print and digital sources, using advanced searches effectively; assess the strengths and limitations of each source in terms of the task, purpose, and audience; integrate information into the text selectively to maintain the flow of ideas, avoiding plagiarism and overreliance on any one source and following a standard format for citation.

Continued

Table A.2. (*continued*)

Common Core Mathematics	Common Core English/Language Arts (ELA)
	W.11–12.9 Draw evidence from literary or informational texts to support analysis, reflection, and research. W.11–12.9b Apply grades 11–12 Reading standards to literary nonfiction (e.g., "Delineate and evaluate the reasoning in seminal U.S. texts, including the application of constitutional principles and use of legal reasoning (e.g., in U.S. Supreme Court Case majority opinions and dissents) and the premises, purposes, and arguments in works of public advocacy (e.g., The Federalist, presidential addresses)"). W.11–12.10 Write routinely over extended time frames (time for research, reflection, and revision) and shorter time frames (a single sitting or a day or two) for a range of tasks, purposes, and audiences. Speaking and Listening Standards SL.11–12.1a Come to discussions prepared, having read and researched material under study; explicitly draw on that preparation by referring to evidence from texts and other research on the topic or issue to stimulate a thoughtful, well-reasoned exchange of ideas. SL.11–12.1b Work with peers to promote civil, democratic discussions and decision-making, set clear goals and deadlines, and establish individual roles as needed. SL.11–12.2 Integrate multiple sources of information presented in diverse formats and media (e.g., visually, quantitatively, orally) in order to make informed decisions and solve problems, evaluating the credibility and accuracy of each source and noting any discrepancies among the data. SL.11–12.4 Present information, findings, and supporting evidence, conveying a clear and distinct perspective, such that listeners can follow the line of reasoning, alternative or opposing perspectives are addressed, and the organization, development, substance, and style are appropriate to purpose, audience, and a range of formal and informal tasks. Literacy Standards L.11–12.1 Demonstrate command of the conventions of standard English grammar and usage when writing or speaking.

Continued

Table A.2. (*continued*)

	L.11–12.1b Resolve issues of complex or contested usage, consulting references (e.g., Merriam-Webster's Dictionary of English Usage, Garner's Modern American Usage) as needed.
	L.11–12.2 Demonstrate command of the conventions of standard English capitalization, punctuation, and spelling when writing.
	L.11–12.2a Observe hyphenation conventions.
	L.11–12.2a Spell correctly.
	L.11–12.3a Vary syntax for effect, consulting references
	L.11–12.6 Acquire and use accurately general academic and domain-specific words and phrases, sufficient for reading, writing, speaking, and listening at the college and career readiness level; demonstrate independence in gathering vocabulary knowledge when considering a word or phrase important to comprehension or expression.

Table A.3. 21st Century Skills Addressed in STEM Road Map Module

21st Century Skills	Learning Skills & Technology Tools (from P21 framework)	Teaching Strategies	Evidence of Success
21st century interdisciplinary themes	Global Awareness Financial, Economic, Business and Entrepreneurial Literacy Civic Literacy Environmental Literacy	Teachers will direct student attention towards the utility of ideas in geology for society, particularly through the analysis of competing design solutions for mineral resources.	Students will articulate how mineral resources are produced and used in society. Students will explain the potential impact of methods for developing, managing, and using mineral resources.
Learning and innovation skills	Creativity & Innovation Critical Thinking & Problem Solving Communication & Collaboration	Teachers will offer access to data sources and local professionals to help students understand the creativity and critical thinking that is required in science.	Students will collaboratively analyze and synthesize qualitative and quantitative data on mineral resources and show how communities can use develop, manage, and use mineral resources by developing an opinion article and/or website to be published.
Information, media and technology skills	Information Literacy Media Literacy ICT Literacy	Teachers will require the use of and examination of various reliable resources for this project and the development of an opinion article.	Students will critically analyze and synthesize multiple streams of information about mineral resources and develop reasonable conclusions to be presented via an opinion article and/or website. Students will use a variety of reliable resources and cite these resources accordingly in their final product.
Life and career skills	Flexibility & Adaptability Initiative & Self-Direction Social & Cross Cultural Skills Productivity & Accountability Leadership & Responsibility	Teachers will provide check points for students to self-monitor their progress.	Students will articulate their goals for each check point for the project and devise strategic plans to show progress toward their goals. Students will work effectively in collaborative groups and be clear about roles of each member.

Table A.4. English Language Development Standards Addressed in STEM Road Map Module

English Language Development Standards: Grades 9–12 (WIDA, 2012)

ELD Standard 1: Social and Instructional Language
    English language learners communicate for Social and Instructional purposes within the school setting.
ELD Standard 2: The Language of Language Arts
    English language learners communicate information, ideas and concepts necessary for academic success in the content area of Language Arts.
ELD Standard 3: The Language of Mathematics
    English language learners communicate information, ideas and concepts necessary for academic success in the content area of Mathematics
ELD Standard 4: The Language of Science.
    English language learners communicate information, ideas and concepts necessary for academic success in the content area of Science
ELD Standard 5: The Language of Social Studies
    English language learners communicate information, ideas and concepts necessary for academic success in the content area of Social Studies.

INDEX

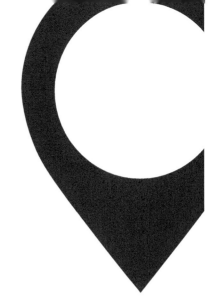

Page numbers in *Italics* represent Figures
Page numbers in **Bold** represent Tables

For Product Safety Concerns and Information please contact our
EU representative GPSR@taylorandfrancis.com Taylor & Francis ASSOCIATION
Verlag GmbH, Kaufingerstraße 24, 80331 München, Germany